living
free

LEARNING TO PRAY
GOD'S WORD

BETH MOORE

LifeWay Press®
Nashville, Tennessee

ISBN 978-1-4300-4330-0
Item 005757874

Dewey Decimal Classification: 248.32
Subject Heading: Prayer\Christian Life

To order additional copies of this resource: write LifeWay Church Resources Customer Service; One LifeWay Plaza; Nashville, TN 37234-0113; email *orderentry@lifeway.com;* fax order to
615.251.5933; phone 800.458.2772; order online at *www.lifeway.com;* or visit the LifeWay Christian
Store serving you.

Printed in the United States of America

Adult Ministry Publishing
LifeWay Church Resources
One LifeWay Plaza
Nashville, TN 37234-0152

CONTENTS

ABOUT THE AUTHOR

Beth Moore has written best-selling Bible studies on the patriarchs, Esther, Moses, Paul, Isaiah, Daniel, John, David, Jesus, and James. *Breaking Free, Praying God's Word,* and *When Godly People Do Ungodly Things* have all focused on the battle Satan is waging against Christians. *Believing God, Loving Well,* and *Living Beyond Yourself* have focused on how Christians can live triumphantly in today's world. *Stepping Up* explores worship and invites us to reach a new level of relationship and intimacy with God.

Beth and her husband, Keith, are devoted to the local church and have the privilege of attending Bayou City Fellowship in Houston, Texas, where their son-in-law Curtis Jones pastors. Beth believes that her calling is Bible literacy: guiding believers to love and live God's Word. Beth has a passion for Christ, a passion for Bible study, and a passion to see Christians living the lives Christ intended.

Beth loves the Lord, loves to laugh, and loves to be with His people. Her life is full of activity, but one commitment remains constant: counting all things but loss for the excellence of knowing Christ Jesus, the Lord (see Phil. 3:8).

Much like Beth, Julie Woodruff, writer of the leader guide material, realized a call from God to ministry while she was a sophomore in college. Over the years that calling has taken the shape of youth ministry and now women's ministry.

Julie is Women's Minister at Long Hollow Baptist Church in Hendersonville, Tennessee. Julie's passion for women's ministry at Long Hollow is to help women find forgiveness and freedom in Christ, to be forged into the likeness of Christ, and to become a force for Christ in the world. She is a graduate of Louisiana College and Southwestern Baptist Theological Seminary.

INTRODUCTION

I recently had a conversation with a young woman named Sarah. She was studying *Breaking Free: The Journey, The Stories.* She was so frustrated with her Christian life, desperately wanting to please God, but she felt He was not pleased with her. Sarah told me that she had struggled with anorexia, so I asked if she is a perfectionist. Of course she said yes.

Sarah wants to be perfect for God. She thinks perfection means that she should never sin. When she does sin, she gets mad at herself for being so unspiritual. Sarah told me that for years she has gone through a cycle of commitment to God, failure, anger at herself, and despair. Not surprisingly, she has been baptized several times. She is obviously a sincere young woman, desperately seeking to please God while focused on her own sin and inadequacy. Sarah has never examined her basic beliefs about God and the Christian life. Like most others, she believes God can be pleased with human performance. Though her ideas are dressed up in biblical language, they are not unlike those of the worshipers of the Canaanite god of fire called Molech. The ancient worshipers thought they could please and manipulate God by burning their children as sacrifices. I am afraid many Sarahs think they can accomplish the same goals by burning themselves on some altar.

In this study I want to propose a different approach to all the Sarahs of this world. We are going to explore the somewhat-radical idea that we cannot please God by being perfect. Even if we achieved the impossible goal of human perfection, we would be not-an-inch closer to pleasing Him. What's more, we cannot please God by focusing on our sins and inadequacies. Won't work. Never happen. Never has. Never will. The only focus that will change our lives is a steady gaze Godward. The more we see Him, the less we will see ourselves. Conversely, the more we obsess over our sin, the more we crowd the Savior out of our sight.

So how do we develop a Godward focus for our lives? I want to propose a two-part answer. One part involves how we see the life God desires for His children. We will explore five benefits God supplies us by His grace. We want to see these five benefits as snapshot-photographs of the life the Father has planned for us. We want to become so familiar with these benefits that we will come to desire to live the life pictured in the photos.

The second part of the answer involves prayer and Bible study. I believe the words of Psalm 107:20, "He sent forth his word and healed them." I believe a connection exists between God's Word, prayer, and a changed life. In this study we want to get practical—to the nuts and bolts—on the matter of pleasing God. How can we overcome persistent, defeating, devastating patterns of sin in our lives? How can we become so non-self-centered that we no longer focus on our own performance? How can we become so God-centered that we no longer want to pursue things that displease Him?

You will find this study linked to two of my previous works, *Praying God's Word* and *Breaking Free. Praying God's Word* seeks to encourage you to connect the two "sticks of dynamite" of prayer and Scripture. In this study I want to help you practice praying God's Word. If you have participated in the study called *Breaking Free*, you will find this study to be a follow-up. We want to get even more practical. If you have not done *Breaking Free*, I think you will find this a useful introduction to that longer Bible study. Either way, I hope you will join me on this journey. We want to grow in our calling: to be displays of His splendor.

NOTE: I have used several resources for study of Greek and Hebrew words. Definitions taken from *The Complete Word Study Dictionary: New Testament* and the *Lexical Aids*[1] are enclosed in quotation marks with no reference. I have also used *Strong's Exhaustive Concordance of the Bible.*[2] Words taken from *Strong's* are enclosed in quotation marks with the word *Strong's* in parentheses.

---

1. Spiros Zodhiates et al., eds., *The Complete Word Study Dictionary: New Testament* (Chattanooga, TN: AMG Publishers, 1992).
2. James Strong, *Strong's Exhaustive Concordance of the Bible* (Madison, N.J., 1970).

Week 1

demolishing strongholds

day one

A MIGHTY FORTRESS

God amazed me with people's response to *Breaking Free: The Journey, The Stories.* The reception confirmed that Christians are struggling with powerful strongholds. Then God led me to write *Praying God's Word.* I have since been asked more questions about Christian liberty. So in this study I want to take some of the content from both *Breaking Free* and *Praying God's Word,* put them together, and help us apply those concepts to our lives.

With my lips I recount all the laws that come from your mouth (Ps. 119:13).

The term *stronghold* appears in the Old Testament almost 50 times but only once in the New Testament. We need to start with the Old both to lay a foundation and to see an important truth to guide us. The Israelites hid from their enemies in strongholds, meaning a "fortress with difficult access" (Judg. 6:2; 1 Sam. 23:14). David and others naturally compared their physical experiences with fortified strongholds to their spiritual experiences with the Lord.

Read Psalm 27:1. Who or what does this passage claim as a stronghold?

□ power   □ the Lord

□ riches   □ sin

What did David conclude since the Lord was his stronghold?

□ **Nothing could physically injure him.**

□ **He would never encounter difficulty.**

□ **He did not have to be afraid.**

The LORD is my light and my salvation—whom shall I fear? The LORD is the stronghold of my life—of whom shall I be afraid? (Ps. 27:1).

Christ as our stronghold does not mean life will be easy or trouble free, but rejoice with me that we do not have to live in fear. God's purposes may lead us to the path of suffering, but wherever He leads, we know He protects. He may protect from suffering or through suffering, but the more we know Him, the less we need to fear.

The LORD is my rock, my fortress and my deliverer (2 Sam. 22:2).

I love what one of my sources said about the Hebrew word for *fortress* in 2 Samuel 22:2. The word used is *misgav,* which means "refuge, stronghold." It comes from a Hebrew word meaning "to be too strong for; to be lofty, be exalted; to lift high; to protect; to be kept safe." What problems do you have that are too strong for God? Do you see Him as lofty and exalted?

Describe a time when God kept you safe.

Have you watched children playing keep-away? Or, if you love basketball as I do, think of a tall player keeping the ball out of an opponent's grasp. That pictures the phrase "to lift high; to protect."

Oh, beloved, let us never lose sight of the protecting stronghold of God. In this study we will confront satanic strongholds, but never forget they are lies. Only the Lord God is the truth. He is our greatest stronghold. How often do you suppose He lifts and protects us? Join me in praying that our precious Father will teach us to see His sheltering hand even when that hand takes us through difficult circumstances.

The LORD will roar from Zion and thunder from Jerusalem; the earth and the sky will tremble. But the LORD will be a refuge for his people, a stronghold for the people of Israel (Joel 3:16).

In this study we're going to pray God's Word. See page 9 for specific help on ways to pray God's Word.

Start by writing your own prayer praising God for being our stronghold. Use the last words of Joel 3:16 to begin your prayer.

HOW DO WE PRAY GOD'S WORD?

How do we learn to pray God's Word? Simply put, praying God's Word means speaking His language. It means talking to Him using His words. Don't waste time looking for a "formula" or "right" way to pray God's Word back to Him. This process comes from what is in your heart and on your mind.

To get you started on this road, I will share my approach. Whenever you read your Bible, watch for passages to talk with the Father about. Especially be on the alert for any Scripture that reflects the mind of Christ toward strongholds in your life. When you are struggling with a specific issue, use a Bible concordance or topical Bible resource to search for Scriptures pertaining to your need. You may not find a detailed description of your stronghold in Scripture, but you will definitely find verses that apply. Ask God to guide you (Ps. 25:4-5) and to open your eyes to His Word (Ps. 119:18). If you're not sure how to use Bible resources like a concordance, ask someone to help you.

When a passage speaks to you, it's time to pray God's Word. You can reword the passage into a prayer in any way God leads you. Here are some examples. I have referenced the passages involved.

1. **Restate God's truth, affirming your faith:** *Father, thank You that You are always good and that Your love endures forever* (1 Chron. 16:34).

2. **Talk to God about passages you don't understand:** *Father Your Word says, "Whoever claims to live in him must walk as Jesus did"* (1 John 2:6). *I know that I do not live up to that standard. Please help me understand and walk like Christ.*

3. **Ask God for what you need:** *"'I do believe; help me overcome my unbelief!'"* (Mark 9:24).

4. **Confess sin and ask God to change your life:** *Father, I know that You hate pride and arrogance* (Prov. 8:13); *yet I see the ugly face of pride in my life. Teach me today to be compassionate and humble* (1 Pet. 3:8).

5. **Praise God with your paraphrase of the words of Scripture:** *I know, LORD, that You are indescribably great. You are greater than all the gods of this world* (Ps. 135:5).

I intend these examples to help get you started in praying God's Word. Please understand that your process won't and doesn't need to look like mine. I am only a fellow sojourner with you—not an expert. Your relationship with the Lord is unique. As you practice and become more comfortable with Scripture-prayer, your method will take on more of your personality and reflect more of your intimate relationship with the Lord.

As you get started, remember that through God's Word and prayer we are equipped with the divine weapons He has given us to demolish strongholds. The goal is abundant life, and God can liberate anyone!

Father, thank You for always being my refuge and stronghold ...

_____

_____

_____

_____

_____

_____

_____

_____

_____

_____

We demolish arguments and every pretension that sets itself up against the knowledge of God, and we take captive every thought to make it obedient to Christ (2 Cor. 10:5).

Unfortunately, God is not the only stronghold available to the children of Adam. Since sin entered the race, we have been mass-producing strongholds with the capable assistance of the evil one. Thus in Scripture we see the word *stronghold* applied both to substitutes for God and the bondage they produce.

The apostle Paul explained strongholds in 2 Corinthians 10:5. Basically, a stronghold is any argument or pretension that "sets itself up against the knowledge of God." The wording in the King James Version draws a clearer image of a stronghold. A stronghold is anything that exalts itself in our minds, pretending to be bigger or more powerful than our God. It steals our focus and causes us to feel overpowered. Controlled. Mastered.

Casting down imaginations, and every high thing that exalteth itself against the knowledge of God, and bringing into captivity every thought to the obedience of Christ (2 Cor. 10:5, KJV).

Whether our stronghold is an addiction, unforgiveness toward a person who has hurt us, or despair over a loss, it consumes so much of our emotional and mental energy that it strangles our abundant life. Our callings remain unfulfilled, and our believing lives become ineffective. Needless to say, these are the enemy's precise goals.

Review the paragraph you just read. Underline the definition of a stronghold and circle statements that describe what a stronghold does.

Did you note that a stronghold is anything that exalts itself in our minds, pretending to be bigger or more powerful than our God? Among other things did you circle that a stronghold steals our focus?

The word *stronghold* appears only once in the New Testament, but other passages convey the same idea. From your Bible carefully read 2 Corinthians 10:3-5. These will be our theme verses for the study. We will examine our weapons (v. 4) later. For now let's consider verse 5. Paul says we are to "demolish arguments and every pretension that sets itself up against the knowledge of God."

Satanic strongholds invade our lives whenever we allow something to appear bigger than God. As we end this first day of study, burn into your heart the fact that strongholds come from false ideas. Though we must deal with demonic strongholds, we can be encouraged when we remember that they are only lies and deceptions.

day two

THE PRIMARY BATTLEFIELD

It is for freedom that Christ has set us free. Stand firm, then, and do not let yourselves be burdened again by a yoke of slavery (Gal. 5:1).

When Satan wages war against us, the primary battlefield is the mind. Second Corinthians 10:5 states the goal of our warfare—to steal back our thought lives and instead take them captive to Christ. The enemy's chief target is the mind because the most effective way to influence behavior is to influence thinking. Our minds are the control centers of our entire beings.

We can easily take a wrong turn on the path to freedom. See if this sounds familiar to you, because I sure know the territory. We struggle with a pattern of thoughts, words, or actions. We promise ourselves that we'll never do it again. We even genuinely hate the behavior involved. Then we hear those hated words come out of our mouths or realize we've done it again, and we feel like pond scum.

In this process we often make a basic mistake. We assume our behavior is the battlefield and the goal is to change our actions.

When the enemy wages war against us, the primary battlefield is the mind.

Why do you think the battlefield is the mind rather than actions?

How do you react to the following statement?
We act out what we believe, not what we know.
□ agree   □ agree but can't quite
□ disagree   explain why

Print the following in your brain and underline it three times: *When the enemy wages war against us, the primary battlefield is the mind.* On a simple basis the battlefield is the mind because our minds control our actions. We decide what we do, but at a deeper level we act out what we really believe. The enemy knows far better than we do that nothing is bigger or more powerful than God, but if Satan can get you to believe his lies, he wins.

Satan lost all rights to presume authority over a believer's life at the cross (Col. 2:13-15). Christ disarmed the forces of evil. He stripped the powers and authorities just as a conquered army was stripped of weapons and armor and put to public shame. Paul wrote that God (in Christ) "made a public spectacle of them." He exposed them to the universe as his captives. Satan is not only a defeated foe; he is a foe who has been publicly humiliated before the hosts of heaven.

Unfortunately, Satan does a remarkable job of making us believe he still has power. He is very good at his job because he's had so much experience. But repeat after me: nothing is bigger or more powerful than God! Absolutely no thing! Not even the strongest addiction or overwhelming feeling of rage. One purpose of this book is to help you downsize anything that has a hold on you until you, in effect, have commanded it to bend the knee to the authority of Christ. Is this really possible? You bet it is!

In the margin circle the key words that appear more than once in 2 Corinthians 10:3-5.

Did you note the words *world, weapons,* and *demolish* each appear twice? We'll specifically examine our weapons in day 4. The word "world" (NIV) or "flesh" (KJV) is *sarx,* and it means "flesh, body, the soft tissue of a creature, often in contrast to bone, ligament, or sinew; by extension human, humankind, with a focus on the fallen human nature." Verse 3 says we live in the *sarx. Live* means "to walk (around); to live, conduct one's life." Since the fateful day when Adam and Eve disobeyed God in the garden, every human being but one has walked around in *sarx*—a sinful, fallen, human nature.

What does 1 John 1:8 tell us about who is without sin?

Hebrews 4:15 appears in the margin. Circle the basic fact that sets Jesus apart from all other human beings.

Though we live in the world, we do not wage war as the world does. The weapons we fight with are not the weapons of the world. On the contrary, they have divine power to demolish strongholds. We demolish arguments and every pretension that sets itself up against the knowledge of God, and we take captive every thought to make it obedient to Christ (2 Cor. 10:3-5).

We do not have a high priest who is unable to sympathize with our weaknesses, but we have one who has been tempted in every way, just as we are—yet was without sin (Heb. 4:15).

I don't propose to understand the mysteries of the Trinity, the virgin birth, or how Jesus could combine being fully God and fully human, but I rejoice in the words "without sin." Since the beginning of time, only one human being has lived free from the *sarx* nature. Paul calls Him the second Adam. "As in Adam all die, so in Christ all will be made alive" (1 Cor. 15:22).

God started a new lineage when Jesus became a human. At the cross Jesus made that lineage available to you and me.

Look back at the repeated words in 2 Corinthians 10. Paul twice used the word "demolish." He used the word *kathairesis,* which is the combination of *kata,* meaning "against, contrary to, opposed," and *haireomai,* meaning "to choose."

> **What clue do you see in the meaning of Paul's word, *kathairesis,* for how we destroy "arguments and pretension"?**

How can we "tear down" lies and false arguments? The answer seems too simplistic. We must choose truth.

> **If the issue is truth versus lies, where is the battlefield?**
> ☐ actions/behavior   ☐ thoughts/beliefs
> ☐ emotions/feelings

Carefully understand that the apostle did not say choose a better course of action. He didn't say choose to do right. We will find that strongholds have far too much fortification for those options. We will find liberty in another way. We must choose truth to tear down Satan's lies. Tomorrow we will consider why human effort cannot accomplish that purpose.

How can we "tear down" lies and false arguments? We must choose truth.

Read Joshua 24:15. Use Joshua's words as the basis for your own written prayer.

Father,

_____

_____

_____

_____

_____

_____

_____

_____

_____

_____

_____

_____

_____

_____

_____

_____

_____

_____

_____

_____

_____

_____

_____

_____

_____

_____

_____

_____

If serving the LORD seems undesirable to you, then choose for yourselves this day whom you will serve, whether the gods your forefathers served beyond the River, or the gods of the Amorites, in whose land you are living. But as for me and my household, we will serve the LORD (Josh. 24:15).

day three

WHAT'S WRONG WITH HUMAN EFFORT?

"My thoughts are not your thoughts, neither are your ways my ways," declares the LORD (Isa. 55:8).

A precious friend came through a time of disobedience, conviction, and repentance. She experienced both genuine brokenness and satanic accusation. After many weeks of deep depression she told me: "I thought I couldn't come to God with this sin in my life. I thought I had to get myself out of the situation before God would have anything to do with me. I didn't feel that He could love me because of what I had done." I wanted to cry at her unbiblical view of God. She fell for the fundamental belief of all pharisees—that God's love is based on our performance. On the contrary, God most wants us to come into His presence in the middle of our times of defeat.

You foolish Galatians! Who has bewitched you? Before your very eyes Jesus Christ was clearly portrayed as crucified. I would like to learn just one thing from you: Did you receive the Spirit by observing the law, or by believing what you heard? (Gal. 3:1-2).

God accepting us depends on ...?
☐ **our obedience to His rules**   ☐ **the sacrifice of His Son**
  ☐ **church attendance**   ☐ **being baptized**

We are so like the Galatians. We continue to believe that God loves conditionally. We cannot believe He operates differently than we do.

Isaiah 55:8 tells us we do not resemble God in our thoughts and ways. The word "thoughts" is *maschashava*. It means "thought, plan, scheme, plot, design." The word "ways" is *derekh*. It means "way, path, route, road, journey; by extension: conduct, way of life." If our thoughts, plans, schemes, and plots aren't like God's, we can bet our ways, paths, and routes won't be either.

Look at those definitions. Just how different do you think our thought process is from God's?

1%	25%	50%	75%	100%

Human intuition points us to what just seems right, but the things of God are seldom intuitive. In fact, often you would be better to figure out what comes naturally and then do the opposite.

> **What word do you find in 1 Corinthians 1:18-25 that most nearly describes our human way of thinking? (If you need a hint, check 1 Corinthians 3:19.)**

Six times in 1 Corinthians Paul described human wisdom as foolishness. We get the English term *moron,* meaning "mentally defective" from the Greek term for *foolishness.* When we follow our instincts with God, we make morons of ourselves.

Let me show you a wonderful example. A vast army came against Judah. Messengers told king Jehoshaphat that the army was already at his southern border. Jehoshaphat consulted a prophet of God and then obeyed some rather strange battle plans.

> **From your Bible read 2 Chronicles 20:20-30 and describe the king's battle strategy.**

If our thoughts, plans, schemes, and plots aren't like God's, we can bet our ways, paths, and routes won't be either.

Would you ever naturally arrive at sending the choir instead of the army out to fight a war? Don't answer if you just had a fight with the minister of music!

> **Can you cite some other examples when God acted in ways opposite to what humans naturally expect?**

I'd love to hear some of your answers. You could fill a book with examples from choosing a shepherd boy to be king to having the Son of God born in a stable. Without a doubt, one example excels them all. Paul calls it the foolishness of the cross.

Since the day sin damaged all areas of human life, we have been re-making the Creator in our own image. We think He acts, feels, and thinks the way we do. We have reality turned completely upside down. He intends for us to act, feel, and think the way He does.

Scripture presents the radical truth that God loves us completely, apart from our actions. Let me give you two examples.

First, if He must punish us because of our stubbornness, He does so in absolute love. All that God does is love because He is love (see 1 John 4:8). You see, God loves even those who go into eternity rejecting Him. That does not question the reality of hell or the tragedy of those who go there. Possibly what will make hell so terrible is the full reality of having rejected God's love.

My second example of God's love relates to prayer. We naturally think if God answers a prayer or grants a miraculous healing, it is because He loves us. If we pray and the answer is no, we question God's love. But beloved, healing or answered prayer has absolutely nothing to do with whether He loves you. It has to do with God's purposes and plans for your life.

When circumstances tempt you to question God's love, learn to look to the right place. John 13:1 tells us: "It was just before the Passover Feast. Jesus knew that the time had come for him to leave this world and go to the Father. Having loved his own who were in the world, he now showed them the full extent of his love."

Where did Jesus show us the full extent of His love?

If your answer included the cross, you have it right. When you wonder about God's love, look to an old rugged cross. Don't look to circumstances. I hope you get my point today. In this matter of freedom we must abandon the belief in human effort. We can never please God by how hard we try. We can never work hard enough to break free from the death grip of sin. A friend said it this way: "If the cross doesn't make God happy, you're not going to make God happy."

Finally, put today's truth in context. Does that mean we need to become spiritual couch potatoes? Should we just sit and wait for God to set us free? The answer is just as "absolutely not" as to the question of human effort. Hebrew 4:11 says, "Let us, therefore, make every effort to enter" God's rest. Second Peter 3:14 tells us to "make every effort to be found spotless, blameless and at peace with him." In both of those Scriptures the word for "effort" is *spoudazo.* It means "to be eager, make every effort, do one's best." As we continue we're going to see how we can do our best to follow hard after Jesus Christ—without relying on human effort.

I told you God's thoughts are not ours. Beloved, it is going to be so much fun learning to follow Him in His power instead of ours!

End today's study by praying through Psalm 86.

day four

THE WEAPONS OF OUR WARFARE

Fight the good fight of the faith. Take hold of the eternal life to which you were called when you made your good confession in the presence of many witnesses (1 Tim. 6:12).

Second Corinthians 10:3-5 identifies four vital details about the weapons of our warfare.

1. They are not the weapons of the world.
2. They have divine power.
3. They are associated with the knowledge of God.
4. Their purpose in warfare is to take our thoughts captive.

Yesterday we saw that the human wisdom will never bring about the liberated life Christ intends for His children. Now let's consider the next detail: the weapons God provides have divine power.

> **Read Ephesians 6:13-18. What offensive weapon does Paul mention?**
> □ belt   □ shoes
> □ shield   □ helmet
> □ breastplate   □ sword
>
> **How is the sword of the Spirit clearly identified?**

The weapons we fight with are not the weapons of the world. On the contrary, they have divine power to demolish strongholds (2 Cor. 10:4).

Paul listed the whole armor of God. Only one piece of the armor is actually a weapon. The figurative belt, shield, breastplate, shoes, and helmet are all defensive pieces of armor intended to keep us from harm. The sword of the Spirit, clearly identified as the Word of God, is the only offensive weapon listed in the whole armor of God.

> **Look again at 2 Corinthians 10:4. What does the plural word weapons suggest to you?**

If you said, "It suggests the existence of another offensive weapon," we are on the same page. Second Corinthians 10:4 uses the plural, assuring us we have more than one offensive weapon for warfare. So we must ask what is the other primary weapon?

In the Ephesians 6 passage, what immediately follows "the sword of the Spirit, which is the word of God"?

Perhaps additional weapons might be identified elsewhere, but the other primary weapon appears right after the words identifying the sword of the Spirit. The next verse says, "Pray in the Spirit on all occasions." I am convinced that the two major weapons with divine power in our warfare are the Word of God and Spirit-empowered prayer.

The two major weapons with divine power in our warfare are the Word of God and Spirit-empowered prayer.

These two weapons have divine power (2 Cor. 10:4). The original Greek word for *power* is the adjective form of the term *dunamai,* meaning "to be able." It is the achieving power of God applied. Perhaps this Greek term might pack a little more punch if we meditated on the fact that our English word *dynamite* comes from the same root word.

Stick with me here, because this is important. Virtually nothing we come against has more power than a stronghold. The very nature of the term tells us that whatever it is, it has a "stronghold" on us. Strongholds can't be swept away with a spiritual broom. We can't fuss at them and make them flee. We can't ignore them until they disappear. Strongholds are broken one way only.

What does 2 Corinthians 10:4-5 tell us must be done to strongholds?
☐ nip them in the bud   ☐ demolish them
☐ starve them to death   ☐ grit your teeth and
                                               do better

The weapons we fight with are not the weapons of the world. On the contrary, they have divine power to demolish strongholds. We demolish arguments and every pretension that sets itself up against the knowledge of God, and we take captive every thought to make it obedient to Christ (2 Cor. 10:4-5).

Have you ever seen a building demolished? The most common way to demolish a modern "fortress" is by deliberately and strategically placing dynamite in the building and then detonating it. Imagine the demolition crew showing up at the building with sticks and stones. They could yell at that building with all their might and throw sticks and stones until they fainted from exhaustion, and it would still be standing. No one would doubt they had tried. They simply had the wrong tools. What they needed was dynamite.

What tools have you used in the past to demolish your strongholds? Check any examples on my list and add your own.

☐ **trying harder**

☐ **punishing myself for failing to live up to God's standards**

☐ **feeling depressed for days over an act of sin**

☐ **promising God I'll do better**

☐ **others:**

You and I are just about as effective as the crew with loud mouths, sticks, and stones when we try to break down our strongholds with carnal weapons like pure determination, secular psychology, and denial. Many of us have expended untold energy trying to topple these strongholds on our own, but they won't fall, will they? That's because they must be demolished.

God has handed us two sticks of dynamite with which to demolish our strongholds: His Word and prayer. What is more powerful than two sticks of dynamite placed in separate locations? Two strapped together. That's what our study is all about: taking our two primary sticks of dynamite—prayer and the Word—strapping them together, and igniting them with faith in what God says He can do. Hallelujah! I'm getting excited just thinking about it!

The ultimate goal God has for us is not power but personal intimacy with Him.

What makes these two sticks of dynamite so powerfully effective when strapped together? Let's consider the stick of prayer first. Prayer keeps us in constant communion with God, which is the goal of our entire believing lives. Prayerless lives are powerless lives, and prayerful lives are powerful lives; but, believe it or not, the ultimate goal God has for us is not power but personal intimacy with Him.

How is intimacy with God different from the goal of being good enough to be acceptable to God?

Yes, God wants to bring us healing, but more than anything, He wants us to know our Healer. Yes, He wants to give us resurrection life, but more than that, He wants us to know the Resurrection and the Life. Please let this truth sink in deeply. It is never the will of God for warfare to become our focus. The fastest way to lose our balance in warfare is to rebuke the devil more than we relate to God. The primary strength we have in warfare is godliness, which is achieved only through intimacy with God. God insists on prayer because His chief objective is to keep us connected entirely to Him.

Review the paragraph above. What develops godliness in a believer?
□ **a regular plan of discipline**   □ **intimacy with God**
□ **keeping rules**   □ **believing right doctrine**

It is never the will of God for warfare to become our focus. The fastest way to lose our balance in warfare is to rebuke the devil more than we relate to God.

We will never win any spiritual battle without prayer, but when the heat of battle has momentarily cooled, the plunder from the battle is a far greater intimacy with God. Prayer is not the means to an end. In so many ways, it is the end itself.

What makes the Word such a powerful stick of dynamite to demolish strongholds? Look once again at 2 Corinthians 10:3-5. Our objectives are to cast down anything that exalts itself in our thought lives and to take our thoughts captive to Christ.

What do you think Scripture means by taking "captive every thought to make it obedient to Christ"?

This is the key I finally recognized after many months of studying these verses. We take our thoughts captive, making them obedient to Christ, every time we choose to think Christ's thoughts about any situation or stronghold instead of Satan's or our own.

Where do we find Christ's thoughts?

I finally learned that the way to make our exalted, overpowering thoughts bow down in obedience to Jesus Christ is to choose to think His thoughts about the matter rather than our own or those influenced by the enemy. The Word of God reveals Christ's thoughts to us.

In my book *Praying God's Word,* I share exactly how I began to think God's thoughts over controlling strongholds in my life. In this study I want to bring together the practice of praying God's Word with the five key benefits from *Breaking Free: The Journey, The Stories.* Then I want to help you use Scripture and prayer so that God can powerfully redirect your life.

Do not conform any longer to the pattern of this world, but be transformed by the renewing of your mind. Then you will be able to test and approve what God's will is—his good, pleasing and perfect will (Rom. 12:2).

In praying Scripture, I not only find myself in intimate communication with God, but my mind is also being retrained, or renewed (Rom. 12:2), to think *His* thoughts about my situation rather than mine. Ultimately, He resumes His proper place in my thought life as huge and indomitable, and my obstacle shrinks. This approach has worked powerfully every time I've applied it. It takes belief, diligence, and time, but the effects are liberating and eternal.

Write a prayer based on Psalm 18:31-35.

_____

_____

_____

_____

_____

_____

day five

KEY YOUR FOCUS

I have a wonderful and a terrible truth for you. We become like the object of our focus. If our focus is on our needs, we become more needy. If our focus is on the harm others have done to us, we become harmful and angry people. If our focus is on material things, we become grasping and greedy. And, praise God, if our focus is on Christ, we become more and more like Him.

Endure hardship with us like a good soldier of Christ Jesus. No one serving as a soldier gets involved in civilian affairs—he wants to please his commanding officer (2 Tim. 2:3-4).

What was the apostle Paul's focus, according to Philippians 3:13-14?

Paul continually emphasized this need for focus. He warned of the dangers of entanglements in 2 Timothy 2:3-4. He declared, "to me, to live is Christ and to die is gain" (Phil. 1:21).

On what does Philippians 4:8 tell us to focus?

Don't mistake Paul's words to be Pollyanna-ish. He's not pushing the power of positive thinking—that if you think about good things, you'll become good. For Paul true, noble, right, pure, lovely, admirable, and excellent are concepts found only in Jesus. He could have said, "Think about Jesus."

What does Hebrews 2:1 tell us to do with the things we have heard (about Jesus)?

In Hebrews 12:2, to whom does the writer encourage us to look?

Peter sends the same signal in 1 Peter 3:15: "Sanctify the Lord God in your hearts" (NKJV). The word *sanctify* means "to set apart, make holy; this can mean active dedication and service to God or the act of regarding or honoring as holy." We sanctify whatever we set apart from the common. Again Peter told us to be "looking for and hastening the coming of the day of God ... looking for new heavens and a new earth" (2 Pet. 3:12-13, NASB).

Describe what specific things you can do to "fix [your] eyes on Jesus, the author and perfecter of [your] faith" and to "sanctify [set apart as holy] the Lord God" in your life.

Remember our definition of a stronghold—anything that exalts itself in our minds, pretending to be bigger or more powerful than our God. To sanctify Christ certainly includes recognizing His absolute uniqueness. Nothing even comes close to challenging Him in power.

In what areas of your life do you need God's power?

He has delivered us from such a deadly peril, and he will deliver us. On him we have set our hope that he will continue to deliver us, as you help us by your prayers. Then many will give thanks on our behalf for the gracious favor granted us in answer to the prayers of many (2 Cor. 1:10-11).

We can easily drift from a pure focus on Jesus. Two of the easiest ways are to become focused on the problems of others or to focus on Satan himself.

Sometimes Satan successfully schemes to keep us in bondage by fueling our focus on others' strongholds rather than our own. We have such a tendency to see the speck in the other person's eye when a log is lodged deeply in ours. I am convinced that as a general rule, strongholds are almost always broken between God and the individual captive. As 2 Corinthians 1:10-11 tells us, we can help others with our prayers, but we cannot fight their battles for them.

We can also become unbalanced in our approach to warfare and strongholds by becoming obsessed with Satan. His utmost goal is to be worshiped (Isa. 14:12-17). Much of worship is focus. Satan wins a tremendous victory and derives much satisfaction when he can get us to focus more on him than on God. That's why this study seeks to center on our communication with God through prayer and His Word far more than give directives on what to say to the devil.

How did Jesus consistently respond to Satan (Matt. 4:1-11)?

Christ set a perfect example for us. We most effectively rebuke Satan when we take our stand in the Word of God. If we know God's Word and how to pray the mind of Christ in a matter, we will be equipped with specific Scriptures when the need arises to face our foe and verbally rebuke him.

The most effective way to live in victory over the devil is to walk in righteousness with God. Strongholds are thoughts taken captive to anything but Christ. If Satan can take our thoughts captive by leading us to focus on battling him, he's successfully built another stronghold.

I often ask God to keep me balanced in the whole counsel of His Word and to help me discern when I'm getting off track. Let's all stay balanced in God's Word. We may be at war with a powerful, unseen enemy, but we are at peace with the Lord God omnipotent, and He still reigns! Now let's consider one last general issue that keeps us focused on Christ.

Remember that God is far more interested in our relationship with the Deliverer than our being delivered. Sometimes the overwhelming power of a stronghold may be instantly broken, but the renewing of our minds takes a lifetime. We demolish strongholds when we make our minds captive to Christ. Let's face it, some holds in our lives are simply stronger than others. If God is getting our full cooperation, the length of the process or the intensity of the struggle is really up to Him. You see, it all depends on His objective. I am certainly no expert, but after about 18 months of researching the biblical topic of strongholds and the Christian, I've come to believe

> We demolish strongholds when we make our minds captive to Christ.

that God generally prioritizes one of two objectives: showing us His power or teaching us that He is all we need.

In the following story underline the part showing God's supremacy and circle the part showing His sufficiency.

I have a sister in Christ whom God set free from an addiction to both alcohol and tobacco years ago. Instantaneously, God broke the stronghold of addiction to tobacco and renewed her mind so that she had no desire whatsoever to smoke. In contrast, she makes the choice to walk in freedom over alcohol addiction almost every day of her life. She still has the desire to drink, although she has lived in victory for many years.

From which stronghold did God set her free? Both! Neither area is controlling her. The instantaneous release from tobacco addiction taught her God's dominion over all things. She saw that nothing is impossible for God. She beheld His absolute supremacy.

However, if God had broken her free of every stronghold that easily and rapidly, she would never have learned to depend on Him. The lingering desire to drink, coupled with an exceeding desire to overcome, has challenged her to choose the authority and power of Christ every single day. In His sovereign wisdom God teaches His strength in her weakness. She has learned God's sufficiency.

The same will probably be true for you and me. Some strongholds will never threaten to take our minds captive again. Others may contest their defeat and demand a rematch every day. Either way God has equipped us to overcome. We are wise not to judge others when they struggle to be free and seem to relapse over and over for a while. None of us is beyond facing the same challenge. Matthew 7:1-2 offers wise counsel when we are tempted to judge a person for his or her inability to attain immediate and lasting victory over a stronghold: "Do not judge, or you too will be judged. For in the same way you judge others, you will be judged, and with the measure you use, it will be measured to you."

Renewing the mind means learning to think new thoughts. That can take some time ... but let's not waste another minute of it, OK? It's time to start igniting some dynamite!

Renewing the mind means learning to think new thoughts.

Week 2

to know God & believe Him

day one

APPLYING THE BENEFITS

For the next five weeks we will focus on the five key benefits God intends for His children. If you have studied *Breaking Free*, you will be familiar with them. In this study we will have an opportunity to explore them more completely. If you have not done that study, here are the five benefits and the central passage from which each comes.

Now that you know these things, you will be blessed if you do them (John 13:17).

God desires for you to:
- ☐ Benefit 1: know God and believe Him (Isa. 43:10);
- ☐ Benefit 2: glorify God (Isa. 43:7);
- ☐ Benefit 3: find satisfaction in God (Isa. 55:2);
- ☐ Benefit 4: experience God's peace (Isa. 48:18);
- ☐ Benefit 5: enjoy God's presence (Isa. 43:2-3).

God gives these gifts to every believer. They are snapshot pictures of what He intends for you to become, five glimpses of God's heart.

Circle the benefit that means the most to you or that you most need in your life right now.

A friend said that of all the material in *Breaking Free*, the five key benefits impacted her most. She said, "The descriptions of God's goals for our lives set me free from a lifelong dilemma. Thinking about breaking free from bondage always stuck me back in a loop. Such considerations always put the spotlight back on me instead of Jesus, and the essence of my struggle has always been a self-focus. Suddenly the five key benefits changed my question from *Am I doing it right?* to *How can I believe God, glorify Him, find satisfaction in Him, experience His peace, and enjoy His presence?*"

"You are my witnesses," declares the LORD, "and my servant whom I have chosen, so that you may know and believe me and understand that I am he. Before me no god was formed, nor will there be one after me" (Isa. 43:10).

What difference do you think it would make in your life to be free from self-centeredness?

☐ It would be incredible.

☐ Sweet relief!

☐ What EVER would I do with my time?

☐ Your response _____

Everyone who is called by my name, whom I created for my glory, whom I formed and made (Isa. 43:7).

We poured the foundation in week 1. Now I'm ready to tell you what I'm really up to in this study. All of us who are moms have surely warned our children not to look directly at the sun. We tell them: "It will put your eyes out." Some things we've told our kids may be old wives' tales, but this one has solid basis in fact. If we look directly at the sun, the lens of the eye focuses the light on our retinas and the image of the sun can literally be burned into our eyes. The last thing we will see is the sun.

Why spend money on what is not bread, and your labor on what does not satisfy?
Listen, listen to me, and eat what is good, and your soul will delight in richest of fare (Isa. 55:2).

I want to turn that physical warning around to make a positive goal. I want us to burn God's five benefits into our spiritual eyes so deeply that they will permanently change our focus. I want us to become so consumed with knowing God, glorifying Him, and finding satisfaction in Him that we will live daily in His peace and presence. I want each of us to get up every morning and go to bed every night with those goals before our eyes.

If only you had paid attention to my commands, your peace would have been like a river, your righteousness like the waves of the sea (Isa. 48:18).

Here are the elements I want to bring together:

• Because the written Word of God expresses the mind of Christ more accurately than anything this side of heaven, we want to think Scripture. Have you noticed that people tend to remember not what goes in their ears but what comes out of their mouths? We think Scripture by using it in our conversations. The most personal and profound form of speech is prayer, when we talk with and listen to God. We want to become so used to talking God's Word with Him that it becomes second nature.

• Because we want to get our eyes off ourselves, our reputations, and our performances, we will concentrate on God's five pictures. The five benefits depict the Spirit-filled life. They show us the character of Jesus and of Christ in us.

I want us to explore these five snapshots until they become burned into our spiritual retinas—to believe God, glorify Him, find satisfaction in Him, experience His peace, and enjoy His presence.

Remember playing with a magnifying glass as a child? Like that glass, the five benefits taken from the Word provide the focus. Prayer tied to God's Word will burn the benefits into our souls.

We're talking pictures here—images. So stop to imagine a bit. What would your life be like if you totally lived within the five benefits? I want you to dream a little.

What would your life be like if you totally believed God?

How would life be different if your greatest desire became to glorify God?

What would it mean for you to find satisfaction in God?

Describe your life if God's peace wrapped around you and protected you even in the midst of the greatest possible turmoil.

What difference would it make if you could perfectly enjoy God's presence with nothing to come between you and Him?

Do those sound like lofty ambitions? I believe they are challenging and worthy but not unattainable. God's intention is for you to live

When you pass through the waters, I will be with you; and when you pass through the rivers, they will not sweep over you. When you walk through fire, you will not be burned; the flames will not set you ablaze. For I am the LORD, your God, the Holy One of Israel, your Savior; I give Egypt for your ransom, Cush and Seba in your stead (Isa. 43:2-3).

every day in those five realities. So how can we get there? In this study we will take several practical steps toward the goal.

- For understanding we will study both the positive and the negative form of each benefit. Sometimes we can better see and understand something by examining its opposite.

- Because we know God's Word has a unity about it, we will take apart and seek to understand related passages that contribute to the same message. Like Ezekiel, we want to "eat" God's Word. To me that means break it down and digest it.

- We will drive these truths into our lives by using God's Word to pray about them.

- Finally, we will take the two sticks of dynamite, the Word and prayer, and we will blow up every stronghold the Devil seeks to build in our lives.

You were shown these things so that you might know that the LORD is God; besides him there is no other (Deut. 4:35).

Let's end this day's study with some Scripture prayer. We will rephrase a passage and then vocalize a prayer. Let me start by giving you an example. Compare Deuteronomy 4:35 to my prayer that follows, and you will see how I have personalized the Word.

Father, I praise You that You have shown me in Your Word many things about freedom so that I may know You are God; besides You there is no other. I now pray that You will show me more of Yourself so that I may know You better (Deut. 4:35).

Now personalize and pray Deuteronomy 7:9.

_____
_____
_____
_____
_____
_____
_____
_____
_____
_____
_____
_____
_____
_____
_____
_____
_____
_____
_____
_____
_____
_____
_____
_____

Know therefore that the LORD your God is God; he is the faithful God, keeping his covenant of love to a thousand generations of those who love him and keep his commands (Deut. 7:9).

day two

BELIEF AND THE BELIEVER

God seems to work in themes in my life. You know what I mean.
Every sermon, morning devotional, and Christian radio program
all "coincidentally" speak to me about the same subject for an
uncomfortable length of time. I'll even get a card in the mail from
a Christian friend I haven't seen in 10 years, and—you guessed it—
she'll share a good word on the exact theme.

Soon after my 40th birthday, everywhere I turned I heard a message
on belief. I'm humiliated to admit that I became somewhat annoyed
not to be hearing more on the subjects I really needed. After all,
I was already a believer, and if believers don't believe, what on earth
do they do?

Several weeks passed, and I still didn't get it. Finally one morning
even Oswald Chambers had the audacity to bring up the subject
in that day's entry of *My Utmost for His Highest.* I looked up and
exclaimed, "What is this all about?" I sensed the Holy Spirit speaking
to my heart, "Beth, I want you to believe Me." I was appalled. "Lord,"
I answered, "of course I believe in You. I've believed in You all my
life." I felt He responded very clearly, adamantly: "I didn't ask you to
believe in Me. I asked you to believe Me."

I sat very puzzled for several moments until I was certain that the
Holy Spirit had faithfully shed light on my pitifully small faith.
I sensed Him saying, "My child, you believe Me for so little. Don't be
so safe in the things you pray. Whom are you trying to keep from
looking foolish? You or Me?"

> **Ouch! Have you been afraid to "put God on the spot" because
> you might look foolish if He didn't come through?**
> □ yes   □ no
> **If so, describe a time when your fear of looking foolish
> controlled your actions.**

I don't mind telling you that my life changed dramatically after God interrupted my comfortable pace with the theme of belief. Some of it has been excruciating, and some of it has been the most fun I've had in my entire Christian life. I have a feeling this is one theme I'll run into again and again in the course of my journey. Why? Because without faith it is impossible to please God. In other words, you and I will be challenged to believe Him from one season to the next, all of our days. If we have even half a heart for God, He's likely to shake our borders and stir up a little excitement.

> **Carefully examine Hebrews 11:6. What does the phrase "that he rewards those who earnestly seek him" mean to you?**

Without faith it is impossible to please God, because anyone who comes to him must believe that he exists and that he rewards those who earnestly seek him (Heb. 11:6).

The writer of Hebrews clearly lays out two requirements of a worshiper of God. First, we must believe that God exists. Without this belief no possibility of faith exists. But belief in God is not enough. After all, the demons can know that sort of faith (Jas. 2:19). There must also be a conviction about God's moral character—belief "that he rewards those who earnestly seek him" (Heb. 11:6). Without that deep conviction, faith in the biblical sense is not a possibility.

> **Place an X to indicate the extent to which you see God as a rewarder.**

●——————————————————————————————————●

Gifts must be pried from Him.

He loves to give.

Don't you see, beloved? You must believe Him. Believe He can do what He says He can do. Believe you can do what He says you can do. Believe He is who He says He is. Believe you are who He says you are.

> **Describe how you would explain to a new believer the difference between believing in God and believing God.**

You may be thinking, *I want to believe! I just don't have enough faith!* God's Word records an encounter in Mark 9:14-24 to encourage every person who wants to believe. Christ met a man with a son who had been possessed by the enemy since childhood. No telling how many physicians, witch doctors, religious fanatics, wise men, and foolish men the father had sought to find freedom for his son.

Imagine the glimmer of hope that kindled this father's soul when rumors circulated about the miracles performed by the disciples of Jesus. Then imagine his devastation when they too were added to the list of the failed.

Jesus asked for the boy to be brought to Him. The father's desperate plea could bring a lump to the throat of any parent: "If you can do anything, take pity on us and help us." I love Jesus' powerful retort: "'If you can?' ... Everything is possible for him who believes." The father's reply represents one of the most honest, priceless moments in the record of Christ's human encounters.

Immediately the boy's father exclaimed, "I do believe; help me overcome my unbelief!" (Mark 9:24).

What two contrasting statements did the boy's father make in Mark 9:24?

I am convinced that God would rather hear our honest pleas for more of what we lack than a host of pious platitudes from an unbelieving heart. When I am challenged with unbelief, I have begun to make the same earnest plea to the One who would gladly supply.

What issue challenges your belief in God's ability or desire to help you?

As we proceed in our study, you will develop your own Scripture-prayers for the purpose of fueling your faith in the One who is faithful and fueling your belief in the One who is believable. I suggest praying such faith-building Scriptures every day.

Remember, God always wills for you to be free from strongholds. We may not always be sure God wills to heal us of every disease or prosper us with tangible blessings, but He always wills to free us from strongholds. You will never have to worry about whether you are praying in God's will about strongholds: "It is for freedom that Christ has set us free" (Gal. 5:1).

Read Ephesians 1:18-20 very carefully. How does Paul describe the "power for us who believe"?
☐ **mighty strength**   ☐ **mighty sword**
☐ **mighty wind**   ☐ **mighty words**

Please accept and celebrate two awesome truths derived from these Scriptures: (1) God wields incomparably great power for those who choose to believe—more than enough to break the yoke of any bondage. Our belief unclogs the pipe and invites the power to flow. (2) God applies the same power to our need that He exerted when He raised Christ from the dead.

Think of any stronghold you face. Does your stronghold require more power than it takes to raise the dead? I don't think so. God can do it, fellow believer. I know because He says so. And I know because He's done it for me. Believe Him … and when you don't, cry out earnestly, *Help me overcome my unbelief!*

End your day's study by writing a prayer based on Ephesians 1:18-20.

Father, I pray that my heart's "eyes" may be …

_____
_____
_____
_____
_____
_____
_____
_____

day three

KNOWING AND BELIEVING

"You are my witnesses,"
declares the LORD, "and
my servant whom I have
chosen,
so that you may know
and believe me and
understand that I am he.
Before me no god was
formed, nor will there be
one after me" (Isa. 43:10).

Isaiah 43:10 says God has chosen His people for two reasons—to know and believe Him. *To know* is the word *yada*. It basically means "to ascertain by seeing." The ancient term included a very personal level of familiarity and was often used to depict the close relationship between a husband and a wife. The term points to the fact that God wants us to know Him intimately through personal experience. He does not want us to settle for secondhand faith.

The word *believe* is *aman*, meaning "to believe, trust, have confidence." The words *yada* and *aman* fit together to say God wants us to trust Him because we know Him intimately. He wants us to have confidence in Him because we have seen Him.

You cannot see my face, for
no one may see me and live
(Ex. 33:20).

We know that no one can physically see God and live (Ex. 33:20). In what sense do you think we can "see" God?

We can't physically see God, but we can see evidences of Him at work. We can associate with people who encourage us to trust Him and who give testimony of His work in their lives.

To the faithful you
show yourself faithful,
to the blameless you
show yourself blameless
(2 Sam. 22:26).

What do 2 Samuel 22:26 and Matthew 5:8 suggest to you about seeing God?

Blessed are the
pure in heart,
for they will see God
(Matt. 5:8).

Name someone you know who gives evidence that they really know God. _____

What about this person is different from other people?

One of your chief purposes on this planet is to know God intimately and with reverent familiarity. That intimate relationship begins— but was never intended to end—with what we call the salvation experience. So the first question to ask yourself is, *Have I received Christ as my personal Savior?* If not, I cannot think of a better time than right now to do so, because Christ is the only entrance to the freedom trail. Turn to page 126 for assistance in how you can place your faith in Christ for salvation.

Did you notice one of the definitions of *believe* in Isaiah 43:10 was the word *trust*? The level of trust we have for God is a monumental issue in the life of every believer. Many variables in our lives affect our willingness to trust God.

> **Briefly identify one life experience that has helped you trust and one that has hindered your ability to trust.**
>
> Helped: _____
>
> Hindered: _____

A loss or betrayal can deeply mark our level of trust. A broken heart, never mended, handicaps us terribly when we're challenged to trust. Trusting an invisible God doesn't come naturally to any believer. A trust relationship grows only by stepping out in faith and making the choice to trust. The ability to believe God develops most often through pure experience: "I found Him faithful yesterday. He will not be unfaithful today."

> **End today's lesson by writing a Scripture-prayer based on Psalm 33:4.**
>
> _____
>
> _____
>
> _____
>
> _____
>
> _____
>
> _____

A trust relationship grows only by stepping out in faith and making the choice to trust. The ability to believe God develops most often through pure experience: "I found Him faithful yesterday. He will not be unfaithful today."

The word of the LORD is right and true; he is faithful in all he does (Ps. 33:4).

day four

THE PERIL OF UNBELIEF

What do you think would be the most obvious obstacle to believing God? As simple as this seems, the largest obstacle is unbelief, choosing not to believe God. We're not talking about believing in God. We're talking about believing God, believing what He says. We can believe in Christ for salvation in a matter of seconds and yet spend the rest of our days believing Him for little more. Eternity can be well secured while life on earth remains shaky at best.

The Greek word for *unbelief* is *apistos*, meaning "not worthy of confidence, untrustworthy ... a thing not to be believed, incredible." We can believe in Christ, accepting the truth that He is the Son of God, and we can believe on Christ, receiving eternal salvation, yet fail to stand firm in belief or choose to find Him trustworthy day to day. The phrase "not worthy of confidence" makes me shudder. God is so deserving of our trust.

Can you think of a time when God proved unworthy of your confidence?

☐ yes   ☐ no   ☐ not sure

Karen's husband was suffering with terminal cancer. Friends told Karen that if she had enough faith, God would heal her husband. When he died, Karen decided God was not to be trusted.

What would you say to Karen about her experience?

If we think we've discovered unfaithfulness in God, I believe we have experienced one of three conditions.

- We misinterpreted a promise from God.
- We missed the answer.
- We gave up before God timed His response.

Karen's well-meaning friends misinterpreted the teaching of Scripture. They assumed faith could make God do what they desired. Unfortunately, Karen came to disbelieve God because of her negative experience. Do you believe God? Or somewhere along the way have you ceased believing God is able?

Now for the good news! If we're willing to admit our lack of confidence in Him, Christ is more than willing to help us overcome our unbelief. Belief—or faith in the abilities and promises of God—is a vital prerequisite for fleshing out our liberty in Jesus Christ.

Believe it or not, I was not always convinced of the absolute dependability of God either—although I never would have admitted it. Not coincidentally, my uncertainty accompanied a sizable lack of knowledge of His Word. I knew what I had been taught and wholeheartedly believed the basics, but I did not become convinced until I really began to study God's Word. Instead of discovering loopholes and worrisome inconsistencies in the Bible, I have been awed to my knees over the beauty of God's Word and the perfect blending of the Old and New Testaments. The study of Scripture has increased my faith at least a hundredfold.

The more you digest God's Word, the more you will find it filled with precious treasures. Let me give you one of about a zillion wonderful examples from Scripture. In Revelation 1:8 the apostle John sees a vision: "'I am the Alpha and the Omega,' says the Lord God, 'who is, and who was, and who is to come, the Almighty.'"

This is what the LORD says–
Israel's King and Redeemer,
the LORD Almighty:
I am the first and I am the
*   last; apart from me there*
*   is no God (Isa. 44:6).*

John got his terms ***alpha*** and ***omega*** from the first and last letters of the Greek alphabet. We use the same idea—from *A* to *Z*. The Old Testament was written in Hebrew, but look at Isaiah 44:6.

> **What message was John conveying about God with the term Alpha and Omega?**
> ☐ The Lord is the only God.
> ☐ The Lord God was here before creation and will be here through eternity.
> ☐ He was speaking of the same God as that of the Old Testament.
> ☐ The Lord is unchangeable, eternally the same.
> ☐ All of the above.

> Next read Revelation 21:6 and compare it to Isaiah 55:1-2. What point do you see John making?

I am the Alpha and the
Omega, the First and the
Last, the Beginning and the
End ... I, Jesus, have sent
my angel to give you this
testimony for the churches.
I am the Root and the
Offspring of David, and the
bright Morning Star
(Rev. 22:13,16).

Do you see that John is tying together the Old and New Testaments? With a few words he shows that Jesus is the fulfillment of the promises of God. He tells us that Jesus is the source of grace and our hope to find genuine satisfaction in life.

> **Finally, by tying together Revelation 22:13 and 16, what does John tell us about the identity of Jesus of Nazareth?**

Do you feel the impact of John's words? If a picture is worth a thousand words, how much are John's majestic images worth? John has shown us so much and capped it off with a declaration that Jesus is the very God who created the universe and who will be here when it has reached its ultimate conclusion.

I feel like a cup bearer at the shore of a crystal clear ocean. I get to return with only one cup of the pure, refreshing water. I hope to tempt you to come and drink for yourself. God wants to use

Scripture in many different ways to feed your faith. As you study the incredible accuracy, detail, and beauty of Scripture, you will come to love Jesus more, and you will feed your faith.

Would you take time to write and pray about your faith? Use these Scriptures and rewrite them into your own prayers. I'll give you an example of my applying God's Word in prayer.

Father, in the parable of the sower, You teach us that the seed of Your Word that falls along the path represents the ones who hear, and then the devil comes and takes away the word from their hearts so that they may not believe (Luke 8:12). Lord, please help me to actively receive Your Word into my heart upon hearing it so that the devil cannot come and take it from me before it has had time to take root.

Luke 24:25

_____
_____
_____
_____
_____
_____
_____
_____

He said to them, "How foolish you are, and how slow of heart to believe all that the prophets have spoken!"(Luke 24:25).

Luke 17:5

_____
_____
_____
_____
_____
_____
_____

The apostles said to the Lord, "Increase our faith!" (Luke17:5).

day five

THE TRUSTWORTHY WORD

Open my eyes that I may see wonderful things in your law (Ps. 119:18).

God has clearly called me to do these Bible studies. I love writing them. I love to research God's Word as He reveals Himself to me in new ways. But I must tell you I am positively horrified by one problem attached to the studies. I never want them to become a substitute for your own relationship with God through His Word.

My soul is weary with sorrow; strengthen me according to your word (Ps. 119:28).

Please promise me you will keep this and every Bible-study book in its proper place—as a mere aid to studying God's Word. I want our time together to help us both draw closer to God through Scripture, but most of all, when you turn the last page, I want you to study and walk with Him apart from this crutch. Even better, as you use this aid, I pray that you will frequently take side trips with the Master.

Consequently, faith comes from hearing the message, and the message is heard through the word of Christ (Rom. 10:17).

In this study we are working on building a communication skill for our relationship with God. Just as wise married couples seek to develop communications skills, we need to build the skill of communicating with God. This particular journey focuses on the skill of praying God's Word back to Him. Because belief is a lifelong issue, we can only begin the process together.

By the time you ought to be teachers, you need someone to teach you the elementary truths of God's word all over again. You need milk, not solid food! Anyone who lives on milk, being still an infant, is not acquainted with the teaching about righteousness (Heb. 5:12-13).

Read the following Scriptures and note what each contributes to the relationship between the Bible and faith.
Psalm 119:28 _____

Romans 10:17 _____

Hebrews 5:12-13 *(also see 1 Peter 2:2)* _____

Like newborn babies, crave pure spiritual milk, so that by it you may grow up in your salvation (1 Pet. 2:2).

Did you note that God supplies strength through His Word, that He actually brings about faith using the Word, and that He feeds our faith with the Word? I can't begin to identify all the ways the Word builds our faith, but let's look at one foundational way.

Second Corinthians 4:13 says, "It is written: 'I believed; therefore I have spoken.' With that same spirit of faith we also believe and therefore speak." If you are in Christ, you have been given that "same spirit of faith."

The original word for *spirit* is literally translated "breath." When you speak God's Word out loud with confidence in Him—rather than your own ability to believe—you are breathing faith. Believing and speaking the truth of God's Word is like receiving CPR from the Holy Spirit.

> Look at another facet of this wonderful jewel called Scripture. Let's look at Old Testament predictions about Jesus. Read the following Scriptures and respond to the instructions about the fulfillment of each.
>
> In what way has the promise of Genesis 18:18 about all nations come to pass?
> □ Abraham established a system of law for all people.
> □ The nation of Israel has provided guidance for all people.
> □ Through Jesus Christ salvation has become possible for all.

Abraham will surely become a great and powerful nation, and all nations on earth will be blessed through him (Gen. 18:18).

You probably noted the fulfillment of the promise to bless all nations points to Christ. Only through the Messiah has the prophecy come to fruition.

> Read Psalm 22 from your Bible. What does the psalm appear to describe?

The psalm describes the experience of the crucifixion hundreds of years before the form of punishment had even been invented. If you want to build your faith, let me give you an assignment. Get a copy of *Nave's Topical Bible.* Look up "Jesus, The Christ.—Prophecies Concerning: Coming of." That will get you started on the three hundred Old Testament prophecies predicting Jesus' coming.

Don't think you can rush out and complete this assignment. It's a lifelong project, but it's also a faith-building project.

Even as I encourage you to build your faith, let me warn you about a false kind of faith. The Pharisees of Jesus' day had a faith, but for many it was a cold, intellectual exercise. Remember that you are studying to build your trust in the author of Scripture, not just to argue about the fact that it's true.

Christ isn't asking us to believe in our ability to exercise unwavering faith. He is asking us to believe that He is able.

In Scripture we clearly see how important trusting the Author can be in the matter of freedom. For example, Matthew 9:27-29 records Jesus' encounter with two blind men. He asked them, "'Do you believe that I am able to do this?' When they said yes, He touched their eyes and told them, 'According to your faith will it be done to you.'"

Please understand. Christ is fully God. He can heal anyone or perform any wonder, whether the belief of the person is great or small. Christ isn't asking us to believe in our ability to exercise unwavering faith. He is asking us to believe that He is able.

When it comes to bringing us to a life of freedom, I believe He is also willing. If we were focusing on physical healing, I would not have such certainty. Sometimes God heals physical sicknesses, and sometimes He chooses greater glory through illness. He can always heal physical diseases, but He does not always choose to bring healing on this earth. Rest assured, however, He created you to be free to love Him. He always desires to see you grow in that freedom.

We have so much more to learn about believing God, but the journey is yours. This feeble effort is just a way to encourage you. Let's end today's study together with my Scripture prayer, and you follow it with one of your own. I'm giving you four passages from which to choose.

> *My Savior, Christ, before You healed the blind men who cried out for Your mercy, You asked them, "'Do you believe that I am able to do this?'" After they replied, "Yes, Lord," You touched their eyes and said, "According to your faith*

will it be done to you" (Matt. 9:28-29). Father, clearly my
faith influences what You are willing to perform in my life.
Please help me believe that You are able.

Now write your Scripture prayer from one of the passages in the margin.

_____

_____

_____

_____

_____

_____

_____

_____

_____

_____

_____

_____

_____

_____

They said to the woman, "We no longer believe just because of what you said; now we have heard for ourselves, and we know that this man really is the Savior of the world" (John 4:42).

"Unless you people see miraculous signs and wonders," Jesus told him, "you will never believe" (John 4:48).

Jesus answered, "The work of God is this: to believe in the one he has sent" (John 6:29).

I have told you now before it happens, so that when it does happen you will believe (John 14:29).

Isaiah 43:10 assures us God wants us to know and believe Him. The most effective key to believing God is right before our eyes: the more we know Him, the more we will believe Him. We tend to run to God for temporary relief. God is looking for people who will walk with Him in steadfast belief. Beloved, choose to believe. Those who trust in Him will not be put to shame.

Week 3

to glorify God

day one

A MIND CAPTIVE TO SELF

What do you think about when you first awake in the morning? I'd like to suggest three possible directions our thoughts can go. Mark 4:19 describes our automatic thoughts before we begin to focus on spiritual things. We find our thoughts captive to "the cares of this world, and the deceitfulness of riches, and the lusts of other things" (KJV). Those describe possibility number one. Before we know Christ, worldly things naturally consume our thoughts.

The worries of this life, the deceitfulness of wealth and the desires for other things come in and choke the word, making it unfruitful (Mark 4:19).

When we come to value the things of the Spirit, we begin to try to please God. We value doing the right things, living up to expectations, being "good" Christians. Such changed values bring us to possibility number two: our thoughts can be centered on pleasing God.

Option number one obviously places the emphasis on pleasing ourselves. On whom does option number two place the spotlight?
□ **God**   □ **others**   □ **ourselves**

Who could object to a goal of pleasing God? Trying to please God can, however, place the spotlight back on ourselves. When our concern centers on how well we live up to expectations, even God's expectations, we find ourselves focusing on ourselves. God wants to change that focus to Himself. I want this third possibility to operate daily in my life. I want to wake up thinking about God's glory instead of my image. I want to think of honoring Him rather than impressing people with me.

What potential problem do you see with the question "How can I live up to God's expectations?"

Remember that pride wears many masks. I once spoke on pride only to have someone remark afterward that she had far too little self-esteem to have pride. She obviously did not understand. Pride is not the opposite of low self-esteem. Pride is the opposite of humility. We can have a serious pride problem that masquerades as low self-esteem. I am convinced that we all struggle with pride issues either thinking too much or too little of ourselves.

> **Which of the following better describes your struggle?**
> ☐ self-centeredness through low self-esteem
> ☐ self-centeredness that I am better than others
> ☐ self-centeredness with both high and low self-worth
> ☐ other response

Humility in the New Testament comes from a root meaning "to lower oneself or to be brought low." Scripture gives us specific guidance to visualize the idea. Just picture Isaiah's vision of God.

"Woe to me!" I cried. "I am ruined! For I am a man of unclean lips, and I live among a people of unclean lips, and my eyes have seen the King, the LORD Almighty" (Isa. 6:5).

> **Restate Isaiah 6:5 in your own words to explain what Isaiah said when he saw God.**

When we see God as He is, we automatically see ourselves as we are. We fall on our faces before His greatness. Low self esteem, as we say in Texas, is a horse of a different color. Low self-esteem means I see myself as low—not because God is great, but because I have so little value.

Don't miss the paradox. When I recognize the greatness of God, I fall on my face before Him, but I also see myself in a new light. Because I am the loved creation of so great a Maker, I cannot help but be a person of great worth.

Low self-esteem has nothing to do with real humility. Pride is self-absorption, whether we're absorbed with how miserable we are or how wonderful we are. Humility is God-focused not self-focused.

We must learn to be constantly on the lookout for pride. We can safely say that if we're not deliberately taking measures to combat pride, it's probably doing something to combat humility. Pride is a monumental boulder in the path toward breaking free.

No matter what stronghold you are seeking to demolish, I suggest praying Scripture about pride every day. We will never waste our time when we pray about our tendency toward pride and seek to humble ourselves before God.

The biggest injustice of pride—it cheats wherever it plays.

I'd like to share a little added initiative to demolishing the stronghold of pride. These are some thoughts God gave me on the subject several years ago. May He use them to speak about the biggest injustice of pride: it cheats wherever it plays.

My name is Pride. I am a cheater.
I cheat you of your God-given destiny ...
because you demand your own way.
I cheat you of contentment ...
because you "deserve better than this."
I cheat you of knowledge ... because you already know it all.
I cheat you of healing ... because you're too full of me to forgive.
I cheat you of holiness ...
because you refuse to admit when you're wrong.
I cheat you of vision ...
because you'd rather look in the mirror than out a window.
I cheat you of genuine friendship ...
because nobody's going to know the real you.
I cheat you of love ...
because real romance demands sacrifice.
I cheat you of greatness in heaven ...
because you refuse to wash another's feet on earth.
I cheat you of God's glory ...
because I convince you to seek your own.
My name is Pride. I am a cheater.
You like me because you think I'm always looking out for you. Untrue.
I'm looking to make a fool of you.
God has so much for you, I admit, but don't worry ...
If you stick with me,
You'll never know.

day two

CREATED FOR HIS GLORY

Everyone who is called by my name, whom I created for my glory, whom I formed and made (Isa. 43:7).

The more I study God's glory, the more convinced I become that it is almost indefinable. Let's look at several Scriptures. However, keep in mind that God's glory far exceeds anything we can comprehend. His glory is everything we are about to learn and infinitely more.

In the next three paragraphs circle the statements describing how God reveals His glory.

First we see that the glory of God always has an impact. Isaiah tells us the seraphim in the throne room of God called to one another: "Holy, holy, holy is the LORD Almighty; the whole earth is full of his glory" (Isa. 6:3, KJV). When Moses and Aaron encountered the glory of God, they fell face down (Num. 20:6). In 2 Chronicles 5:14 "the priests could not perform their service because of the cloud, for the glory of the LORD filled the temple." When God's glory appears, it can't help but interrupt any routine.

God makes Himself known through His glory. Psalm 19:1 says:

> The heavens declare the glory of God;
> the skies proclaim the work of his hands.
>
> **PSALM 19:1**

Psalm 29:9 demonstrates the power of God's self-revelation:

> The voice of the LORD twists the oaks
> and strips the forests bare.
> And in his temple all cry, "Glory!"
>
> **PSALM 29:9**

God's glory is how He shows who He is.

God's glory does not just reflect Him. It's part of who He is! In those references, the Hebrew word for *glory* is *kavodh* meaning "weight, honor, esteem." The word comes from another Hebrew term; *kavedh* means to "be renowned ... to show oneself great or mighty." In other words, God's glory is the way He makes Himself known or shows Himself mighty. God wants to reveal Himself to humans. Each way He accomplishes this divine task is His glory. God's glory is how He shows who He is.

Fill in the blanks to review the key facts about God's glory.
God's glory always has an _____.

God makes Himself _____ through His glory.

God's glory is part of who He _____.

Write your own definition of God's glory.

Read Isaiah 6:1-8 aloud. How did Isaiah's vision of God's glory change how he saw himself?

How do you think it changed how he lived his life?

How has God's glory changed the course of your life?

Isaiah's vision almost destroyed him at first. Seeing God's glory cast the prophet in a whole new light. No longer could he fool himself into believing he was a good man. In the light of God's glory Isaiah was "ruined." The Hebrew word is *damah*, and it means "to perish, be ruined, be destroyed, be wiped out." Every possibility of human goodness suddenly fled away in the presence of God's glory.

Have you thanked God for burning away even the possibility of human goodness? If you are willing to take that attitude to God, use Isaiah 66:2 as the basis for your prayer.

We looked at Old Testament pictures of God's glory. Now consider the following New Testament views of His glory, and note what they add to our understanding.

Read Matthew 16:16-17. How did Peter come to understand Jesus' true identity?

The Word became flesh and
made his dwelling among
us. We have seen his glory,
the glory of the One and
Only, who came from the
Father, full of grace and
truth (John 1:14).

In the same way, if you have come to recognize God's holiness and your own sinfulness, God has revealed it to you. You cannot come to that realization apart from the Holy Spirit, just as you cannot truly call Jesus Lord except through the Holy Spirit (1 Cor. 12:3).

Compare John 1:14 and 2:11. What common thread do you see in the two verses?

Did you note that God revealed Himself? As we continue with our study, we will see God's glory consistently connected to His self-revelation.

> **How do you suppose the apostle Paul came to the following statement in Romans 7:18? "I know that nothing good lives in me, that is, in my sinful nature."**
> ☐ **He had low self-esteem.**
> ☐ **He thought deeply about philosophy and theology.**
> ☐ **He encountered God's glory.**

Christ spoke to the apostle Paul on the Damascus road. God's glory literally knocked him off his donkey.

I asked how God's glory has interrupted your life. You probably have not seen a light that left you blind for three days or heard an audible voice from heaven, but have you come to see that God is holy and that you are unworthy to stand in His presence? That was the Holy Spirit interrupting you with God's glory. Your call does not have to be dramatic like Paul's or Isaiah's to be just as real.

This, the first of his miraculous signs, Jesus performed at Cana in Galilee. He thus revealed his glory, and his disciples put their faith in him (John 2:11).

day three

THE OBSTACLE OF PRIDE

When pride comes, then comes disgrace, but with humility comes wisdom (Prov. 11:2).

If God reveals Himself through His glory, what would be the primary obstacle to my glorifying Him? Sadly, I have a natural inclination to showcase me rather than to reveal Him. Scripture has a name for glorifying myself. It calls this obstacle *pride*. Perhaps no other spiritual obstacle is quite like this one. The challenge to overcome pride may be the only common denominator on every one of our spiritual to-do lists.

How many of your life problems involve your pride?

1%   100%

Think of a personal conflict you have experienced with another person. Write some initials or a code name to pin down the identity.

Now describe the part your pride played in the conflict.

Can you even conceive of a conflict between people that is not pride-based? I don't think I can. A simple reason exists for pride's Goliath proportions: pride is Satan's specialty. It is the characteristic that most aptly describes him. Pride is the issue that had him expelled from heaven. It is still one of Satan's most successful tools in discouraging people from accepting the gospel of Jesus Christ.

Let's not fool ourselves into thinking that pride is a problem only for the lost. The most effective means the enemy has to keep believers from being full of the Spirit is to keep us full of ourselves. No wonder the Bible states and restates that God hates pride. It destroys our usefulness to God. It wrecks lives and destroys relationships.

Let's lose our minds for a moment and imagine our lives if we were completely free from self-glorification. Describe what your life might be like if you never had to struggle with pride. Plan to discuss this in your group meeting this week.

Don't confuse pride with satisfaction over a job well done. If we say, "She takes pride in her work." we might mean something positive as in, "She does her job well to glorify God." Or it might be destructive as in, "She does a good job so that people will like her."

Remember what it means to glorify God. In simple terms, God is glorified in anyone through whom He is allowed to show Himself great or mighty. We live a God-glorifying life by adopting a God-glorifying attitude. God tucked a wonderful Scripture in the Book of Isaiah that beautifully illustrates an attitude through which God will undoubtedly be glorified.

What does Isaiah 26:8 say will be the desire of our hearts?

Yes, LORD, walking in the way of your laws, we wait for you;
your name and renown are the desire of our hearts (Isa. 26:8).

God will show Himself great and mighty in those whose heart's desire is His name and renown. The original word for *renown* is *shem*, which means "definite and conspicuous position ... honor, authority, character ... fame" (Strong's).

Would you join me in praying Isaiah 26:8? Ask God to make His name and renown the desire of your heart. Write your prayer below.

Everyone who is called by my name, whom I created for my glory, whom I formed and made (Isa. 43:7).

According to Isaiah 43:7, we are called to allow the King of all creation to reveal Himself through us. He will not share His glory with another, not even with His own children. God is not egotistical; He's interested in our eternal treasures.

How could God's demand to be the focus of glory be in our best interest?

By demanding that we seek His glory alone, God calls us to overcome the overwhelming and very natural temptation to seek our own. One of the greatest gifts God could possibly give us is to deliver us from our own pride. Alexander Pope called it "the never-failing vice of fools." Pride is a destroyer of ministries, marriages, friendships, jobs, and character.

I am absolutely convinced that seeking God's glory rather than our own incredibly enhances life on a purely human level. The trouble is it can't be done on a human level. Few things are more contrary to our human natures than desiring anyone's fame above our own. When we try in our own power, we grow angry and bitter because we aren't getting the attention we desire. Even when we desire the fame of our spouses or children, deep inside we are often yearning for the fame they might lend to us.

To fulfill our God-given destinies—to allow the King of all creation to show Himself through us—we must overcome the temptation to seek our own glory by desiring His instead. If we are to recognize and allow God to free us from any areas of captivity, we must recognize pride as more than self-promotion. Pride is a dangerous lure to captivity.

day four

DEALING WITH PRIDE

Like the ancient people of Moab in Isaiah 25, we often have high, fortified walls built around the strongholds in our lives. Few strongholds match that of pride. To tear away the stronghold, God must empower each of us to smash the fortress of pride.

He will bring down your high fortified walls and lay them low; he will bring them down to the ground, to the very dust (Isa. 25:12).

The most basic definition of *repent* in the New Testament means "to have a changed mind." We need God to change our minds about pride in three ways.

1. We need to change the way we view pride.
2. We need to change the way we view humility.
3. We need to humble ourselves before God.

In *Breaking Free* I pictured this change as shoving the obstacle of pride from our road to freedom. Consider with me the three shoves we must use to give pride the old heave-ho.

The first shove is to view pride as a vicious enemy. Proverbs 8:13 quotes God saying "I hate pride and arrogance." Proverbs 11:2 proclaims, "When pride comes, then comes disgrace, but with humility comes wisdom." Proverbs 13:10 adds that, "pride only breeds quarrels, but wisdom is found in those who take advice." And most of us are familiar with the words if not the location of Proverbs 16:18: "Pride goes before destruction, a haughty spirit before a fall."

Why do you think God hates pride?

What difference do you see between God's attitude and yours?

Let me see ... God hates it, it brings disgrace, it breeds quarrels, and it points us to destruction like a compass needle seeking north. Obadiah 1:3 caps it all off. "The pride of your heart has deceived you," God said. Though you may dwell in the "clefts of the rocks" and "say to yourself, 'Who can bring me down'... 'from there I will bring you down declares the LORD'" (Obad. 1:3-4). The first order of business to be rid of pride is to view it as the vicious enemy it is.

To fear the LORD is to hate evil; I hate pride and arrogance, evil behavior and perverse speech (Prov. 8:13).

Pray God's Word from Proverbs 8:13 about your view of pride.

The second shove is to view humility as a friend. Often our society reviles biblical humility as a sign of weakness. Nothing could be further from the truth. Being filled with pride comes naturally. Humility takes a supply of supernatural strength that comes only to those strong enough to admit weakness.

Underline the benefits of humility in the next paragraph.

You glimpse the value of humility in that both James and Peter quote Proverbs 3:34, "God opposes the proud but gives grace to the humble" (Jas. 4:6; 1 Pet. 5:5, KJV). Isaiah quotes God saying, "I live in a high and holy place, but also with him who is contrite and lowly in spirit" (Isa. 57:15). And God says, "This is the one I esteem: he who is humble and contrite in spirit, and trembles at my word" (Isa. 66:2). "Esteem" basically means to "have respect" (Strong's). Can you imagine being one whom God respects? What a wonderful thought! To remove the obstacle of pride, we must view it as a bitter enemy and view humility as a dear friend.

Did you note these benefits? God gives grace to the humble. He lives with the humble, and He holds the humble in high esteem. One friend said, "God just likes to hang out with humble people." Wow!

How would you rate your attitude toward humility?

☐ I look down on humble people as weak.

☐ I admire humility when I see it in others.

☐ I want to be a person of humility.

☐ I don't want to have anything to do with humility.

Please talk to the Father based on Proverbs 22:4.

Humility and the fear of the LORD bring wealth and honor and life (Prov. 22:4).

The third and final shove to push over the wall of pride requires humbling ourselves before God. James 4:10 and 1 Peter 5:6 plainly tell us to humble ourselves. You see, humility is not something we have until humbling ourselves is something we do. This step necessitates action before possession. Humbling ourselves certainly does not mean hating ourselves. Humility can be rather easily attained by simply opening our eyes to reality. Just read a few chapters of Scripture boasting in the greatness of God; Job 38 is one of my favorites.

Humility is not something we have until humbling ourselves is something we do.

From your Bible read Job 38. Pick a verse or two to pray back to God.

We certainly don't have to hate ourselves to see how small we are and to respond appropriately by bowing down before Him. In a nutshell, that's what humbling ourselves before God means: bowing down before His majesty. We don't have to hang our heads in self-abasement to humble ourselves. We simply must choose to lower our heads from lofty, inappropriate places. The last sentence of Daniel 4:37 provides one of the most effective motivations for humility in my personal life: "Those who walk in pride he is able to humble."

I look at it this way: I'd rather humble myself than force God to humble me. Let's allow the circumstances, weaknesses, and any thorns in the flesh God has chosen to leave to do the job they were sent to do—provoke humility. Not so we can be flattened under God's doormat, but so He can joyfully lift us up. Take a moment today to find a private place, get down on your knees, and humble yourself before your glorious God. The hosts of heaven are sure to hear a thunderous rumble as boulders of pride roll off our road to freedom.

day five

MAKING GOD RECOGNIZABLE

How can you and I glorify God? Consider the New Testament word for *glory* and note what it adds to our understanding. The Greek word for *glory* is *doxa*. It means "the true apprehension of God or things. The glory of God must mean His unchanging essence. Giving glory to God is ascribing to him His full recognition."

So whether you eat or drink or whatever you do, do it all for the glory of God (1 Cor. 10:31).

Look at Isaiah 43:7 once more: "Everyone who is called by my name, whom I created for my glory, whom I formed and made." Based on what we've learned from our Scriptures and definitions, I believe being created for God's glory means two marvelous truths to those who are called by His name.

- God wants to make Himself recognizable to us.
- God wants to make Himself recognizable through us.

God wants to be recognizable in us in all we do! Living a life that glorifies God is synonymous with living a life that reveals God.

> **Think back to the first person who revealed God to you. What about him or her made God recognizable?**

A life that glorifies God is not something we suddenly attain. As we spend time in God's presence, His glory both transforms us and radiates from us. Paul used the example of Moses' meeting with God to illustrate this practical truth. When Moses had been in the Lord's presence, his face glowed with God's glory so much that Moses put a veil over his face (Ex. 34:33). Paul wrote of Christians: "We, who with unveiled faces all reflect the Lord's glory, are being transformed into his likeness with ever-increasing glory, which comes from the Lord, who is the Spirit" (2 Cor. 3:18).

I hope you didn't miss the fact that we are being changed into Christ's "likeness with ever-increasing glory." I love the King James Version's words: "from glory to glory"!

You see, people who are living out the reality of their liberation in Christ (Gal. 5:1; 2 Cor. 3:17) progress in their spiritual lives in an "ever-increasing glory." As they grow in spiritual maturity, the Spirit of Christ becomes increasingly recognizable in them. Likewise, when Christ is not recognizable in a redeemed life, we need to identify and allow God to treat the area of captivity.

We were created for the purpose of giving God's invisible character a glimpse of visibility. If we grasp all the eternal implications of such a destiny, we would want to do anything possible to make sure all hindrances were removed.

Reflect again on the words of Isaiah 43:7: "Everyone who is called by my name, ... I created for my glory." Allow me to attempt to summarize.

- We were created for God's glory.
- We have no hope of God's glory without the indwelling Spirit of Christ, who comes at our salvation.
- We fulfill what we were meant to be when God is recognizable in us.
- A life that glorifies God or makes Him recognizable is a process that ideally progresses with time and maturity.

You may wonder how a person can recognize whether his or her life is glorifying God. Think about the following Scriptures and statements. They help me to determine whether benefit 2 is a present reality in my life.

Therefore, there is now no condemnation for those who are in Christ Jesus (Rom. 8:1).

Please don't be dismayed if you feel you are not already living a life that glorifies God! He never sheds light on our weaknesses or shortcomings for the sake of condemnation (Rom. 8:1). God makes us aware of hindrances so He can set us free!

Here is my personal checklist of Scriptures and evaluations. I seek to apply these to my life on a regular basis. Look up the Scripture passage, and after each question place a mark where you see yourself.

1. Is my most important consideration in every undertaking whether God could be glorified? (1 Cor. 10:31)

1%   100%

2. Do I desire His glory or my own? (John 8:50,54)

1%   100%

3. In my service to others, is my sincere hope that they will somehow see God in me? (1 Pet. 4:10-11)

1%   100%

4. When I am going through hardships, do I turn to God and try to cooperate with Him so He can use those hardships for my good and for His glory? (1 Pet. 4:12-13)

1%   100%

5. Am I sometimes able to accomplish things or withstand things only through the power of God? (2 Cor. 4:7)

1%   100%

In Christian circles we often use phrases like "totally transformed" or "completely changed." What does the phrase "changed ... from glory to glory" suggest to you about such absolute language?

☐ God changes our lives all at once, one time.

☐ God transforms our lives one step at a time.

☐ God has either changed your life completely or not at all.

None of us consistently glorify God in everything we say and do, but we can experience genuine liberation in Christ. God wants to do more in our lives than we've ever heard, seen, or imagined (1 Cor. 2:9), but He does it one step at a time. God protects us from pride by keeping us somewhat unaware of the degree to which we are effectively glorifying Him at times. However, when we are able to respond that we're making progress, God is being glorified! Just be sure to turn around and give Him the glory!

This unit may have been difficult for you. You may feel that you have a long way to go before you are fulfilling His purpose. Instead, I hope you can see the magnificent potential He planned for you to fulfill. On the other hand, you may be able to celebrate some progress in your pursuit of a God-glorifying life. No matter what God has exposed to you, relish the wonderful words of Christ that pertain to you. From the shadow of the cross, He said of you: "I pray for them. I am not praying for the world, but for those you have given me, for they are yours. All I have is yours, and all you have is mine. And glory has come to me through them" (John 17:9-10).

In this context Christ used the word *glory* to indicate wealth and riches He had received. No matter where you are on the journey to the glorifying, liberated life in Christ, you are His treasure. He does not want to take from you. He wants to give to you and free you from any hindrance.

Please conclude this unit by praying through the following Scriptures. Write your prayers on the lines following each passage.

"As God's chosen people, holy and dearly loved,
clothe yourselves with compassion, kindness,
humility, gentleness and patience."
COLOSSIANS 3:12

_____
_____
_____
_____
_____
_____
_____
_____
_____

"All of you, clothe yourselves with humility
toward one another, because, 'God opposes the
proud but gives grace to the humble.'"
1 PETER 5:5

_____
_____
_____
_____
_____
_____
_____
_____
_____

Week 4

to find satisfaction in God

day one

THE GOD WHO SATISFIES

God intends for the five benefits to become our primary motivations. We have explored two of the five: to believe God and to glorify Him. Next let's consider *benefit 3: to find satisfaction in God.*

You will know the truth, and the truth will set you free (John 8:32).

I believe lack of satisfaction is the hidden scandal of modern Christianity. Though we would not think of admitting it, many Christians are not satisfied with Jesus.

Before you call me a heretic, let me set the record straight: Jesus is absolutely satisfying. In fact, He is the only means by which anyone can find true satisfaction. However, I believe a person can receive Christ as Savior, serve Him for decades, and meet Him face-to-face in glory without ever having experienced satisfaction in Him.

> **What might be some of the evidences of lacking satisfaction with Jesus? If you were a doctor diagnosing an illness, what symptoms would you look for? Plan to discuss your answers with your small group.**

The Bible uses the word *soul* in a number of ways. One of those ways is to refer to the nonmaterial part of us. When I speak of soul hunger, I am referring to our need for spiritual satisfaction. Is your soul, your spirit, your own inmost place, the real you, entirely satisfied with Christ? As we meditate on our answers, let's consider the biblical meaning of satisfaction through several Old Testament Scriptures. Isaiah records God issuing a poetic and classic invitation in chapter 55.

What does God freely offer His people? (Isa. 55:1)

Come, all you who are
thirsty, come to the
waters;
and you who have no
money, come, buy
and eat!
Come, buy wine and milk
without money and
without cost.
Why spend money on what
is not bread, and your
labor on what does not
satisfy?
Listen, listen to me, and eat
what is good, and your
soul will delight in the
richest of fare
(Isa. 55:1-2).

What question does God ask in Isaiah 55:2?

We falsely believe that possessions, power, or people will make us happy. The prophet contrasts the world's attempt to find satisfaction with what God provides. The Hebrew word used for *satisfy* is *sob'ah* meaning "to have enough, be full ... sufficiently" (Strong's). In effect, God is asking, Why do you work so hard for things that are never enough, can never fill you up, and are endlessly insufficient?

We've each been disappointed by something we expected to bring satisfaction. When we seek satisfaction in the wrong places, we not only doom ourselves to failure, but we also become downright dangerous to others. In their neediness some people become like emotional or spiritual vampires. They suck the life right out of others.

Sadly, dissatisfied mates or parents often seek to use spouses or children to try to satisfy the holes in their own souls. We need to get the message clearly through our skulls that God never intended any other earthly relationship to fulfill our deepest needs.

What do you think a truly satisfied person would look like? (Check all the answers that fit.)

□ open   □ fearful
□ happy   □ bitter
□ self-centered   □ optimistic
□ giving   □ patient
□ confident

In the list above, circle the characteristics of a dissatisfied person.

What do you think of when you think of the word *satisfaction*? Describe the most satisfying event you remember experiencing.

Consider how that experience of satisfaction felt. Then multiply it a thousand times and imagine experiencing such desire, delight, and fulfillment in God's presence. He intends all that and more for you.

Do you see the connection between captivity and a lack of satisfaction in Christ? We can easily be led into captivity by seeking other answers to needs and desires only God can meet. Perhaps we have each experienced an empty place deep inside that we tried our best to ignore or to fill with something other than God.

A crucial part of fleshing out our liberation in Christ means allowing Him to fill our empty places. Satisfaction in Christ can be a reality. I know from experience, and I want everyone to know how complete He can make us feel. I'm not talking about a life full of activities. I'm talking about a soul full of Jesus. The filling only He can give does not automatically accompany our salvation. I was in my early 30s before I understood the huge difference between salvation from sin and satisfaction of soul. Salvation secures our lives for all eternity. Soul satisfaction ensures abundant life on earth.

Would you join me in praying the following Scripture-prayer about a soul-satisfying relationship with God?

You, my God, made the world and everything in it. You are the Lord of heaven and earth, and You do not live in temples built by hands. You are not served by human hands as if You needed anything, because You Yourself give all of us life and breath and everything else. From one man You made every nation, that they should inhabit the whole earth; and You determined the times set for them and the exact places where they should live. You, my Father, did

You open your hand and
satisfy the desires of
every living thing.
The LORD is righteous in
all his ways and loving
toward all he has made.
The LORD is near to all who
call on him, to all who
call on him in truth.
He fulfills the desires of
those who fear him;
he hears their cry and
saves them.
The LORD watches over all
who love him, but all the
wicked he will destroy.
My mouth will speak in
praise of the LORD, Let
every creature praise his
holy name for ever and
ever (Ps. 145:16-21).

this so that people would seek You and perhaps reach out
for You and find You, though You are not far from each
one of us. For in You we live and move and have our being!
(Acts 17:24-28)

Write your own Scripture-prayer based on Psalm 145:16-21.

_____

_____

_____

_____

_____

_____

_____

_____

_____

_____

_____

_____

_____

_____

_____

_____

_____

_____

_____

day two

THE HEART'S CRY

We are seeking to develop five images in our minds. These five benefits picture our birthright as children of the King. They describe our Lord Jesus because He certainly lived them out. At a very practical level they can become our life goals and a daily checklist to keep us on the right path. Currently, we are exploring the third benefit. God intends for us to find satisfaction in Him—complete, lasting, soul-quenching, emptiness-filling satisfaction.

In many ways I fear Mick Jagger is the poster child for modern life. "I can't get no satisfaction" rings like an anthem from our society, but the roots go far deeper. You only have to read the words of King Solomon to catch a glimpse of the universal human condition.

> *"Meaningless! Meaningless!" says the Teacher. "Utterly meaningless! Everything is meaningless."*
>
> *"I have seen all the things that are done under the sun; all of them are meaningless, a chasing after the wind" (Eccl. 1:2,14).*

Read Ecclesiastes 1:2,14. Underline Solomon's outlook on life.

The Hebrew word *hevel*, translated *meaningless*, means "breath; by extension: something with no substance, meaninglessness, worthlessness, vanity, emptiness, futility; idol."[1] Now think about it. Solomon had everything. He was possibly the most powerful king on earth at the time. He could certainly have anything he wanted, yet he could "get no satisfaction." He found life to be worthless and futile.

We all want satisfaction. Does Solomon's example challenge any of your assumptions, like the belief that you will finally be happy if only you achieve that next goal?

In the following list underline anything you have sought in the past, thinking it would satisfy your deep inner longing.

job/career	marriage	children	hobbies
money	success	fame	security
reputation	beauty	relationships	control
power	admiration	approval	drugs/alcohol

What would you add to the list that you sought as a source of satisfaction?

Go back and review your list. Place an X over anything you, like Solomon, have tried and found inadequate to satisfy.

Obstacles on our road to freedom:
• unbelief
• pride
• settling for satisfaction with anything else

Review the list one last time. Circle any source of satisfaction you are still seeking.

By the way, it's OK if you both underlined, crossed out, and circled something. I know life can be just that confusing. As long as we're seeking satisfaction in those things, we will be like Solomon, "chasing after wind." Now let's get honest and biblical.

What should we call this grabby process of seeking satisfaction in anything but God?
☐ arrogance   ☐ greed   ☐ idolatry

We have seen that unbelief and pride form the first two obstacles on our road to freedom. Realizing God desires for us to find genuine satisfaction in Him helps us discover the third primary obstacle: *settling for satisfaction with anything else.* God gave this practice a name I was unprepared to hear: idolatry. After serious meditation, I realized the label makes perfect sense, no matter how harsh it seems. Anything we try to put in a place where God belongs is an idol.

You and I as believers in Christ have been chosen to know, believe, and understand that He is God (Isa. 43:10). Our lives have been sanctified by the one true God. Heaven is His throne. Earth is His footstool. The winds do His bidding. The clouds are His chariot. The earth trembles at the sound of His voice. When He stands to His feet, His enemies are scattered. He is transcendent over all things. Absolute. Uncontested. Omniscient. Omnipresent. The Lord God omnipotent reigneth. He is God, and there is no other.

The mystery I will never fully understand is why we would trade God, the only source of genuine satisfaction, for worthless idols that can never satisfy. Yet that transaction calls to you and to me every day of our lives.

Therefore, we need a very simple goal for our satisfaction. We must recognize that God and God alone can satisfy. We must unmask the false gods to which we are drawn. We must confess our unfaithfulness for the idolatry it is and seek Him only. Toward that end we need to use Scripture prayers every day of our lives. The Bible is filled with passages about the Godness of God. These passages feed the truth we need reinforced.

Here is one of my examples. Join me in praying this prayer. Then convert Nehemiah 9:6 into your own prayer.

My Father, I acknowledge that You are the Lord Almighty. You are the first and You are the last, and apart from You there is no other God. Make me witness to the fact that there is no other Rock but You. Enable me to say with full assurance, "I know not one" (Isa. 44:6,8).

Now write your own prayer based on Nehemiah 9:6.

_____
_____
_____
_____
_____
_____
_____
_____
_____
_____
_____
_____
_____
_____
_____

You alone are the LORD. You made the heavens, even the highest heavens, and all their starry host, the earth and all that is on it, the seas and all that is in them. You give life to everything, and the multitudes of heaven worship you (Neh. 9:6).

1. NIV Complete Study Bible

day three

A PICTURE OF SATISFACTION

O God, you are my God,
earnestly I seek you;
my soul thirsts for you, my
body longs for you,
in a dry and weary land
where there is no water
(Ps. 63:1).

We can learn several truths about satisfied souls by drawing a parallel between the soul and the physical body. I know this seems simplistic, but humor me for a moment. How do you know when you are hungry? When you are thirsty?

Continue to humor me here. What do you usually do when you're hungry or thirsty? You seek what will meet your need. If you ignore your physical needs long enough, not only will you be miserable, but you will also be ill.

You can easily recognize the signals the body gives, but great wisdom lies in learning to discern the signals your spiritual nature gives. Psalm 63 offers insight into the satisfied soul. Look how David continued describing satisfaction:

> Because your love is better than life,
> my lips will glorify you …
> My soul will be satisfied as with the richest of foods.
> **PSALM 63:3,5**

The most obvious symptom of a soul in need of God's satisfaction is a sense of inner emptiness. The awareness of a hollow place somewhere deep inside—the inability to be satisfied—ought to be a flashing caution light to every believer.

What clue does Psalm 63:2 suggest about how David developed the capacity to thirst for God?

I have seen you in the
sanctuary and beheld
your power and your
glory (Ps. 63:2).

The soul can also manifest physical symptoms of need. I like to think of it this way: Just as my stomach growls when I'm hungry for physical food, my spirit tends to growl when I'm in need of spiritual food. When a checker at the grocery store seems overtly irritable or grouchy, I sometimes grin and think to myself, *I bet her kids woke her before she had a chance to have her quiet time!* I can certainly assure you that my personality is distinctively different when I haven't had the time I need with the Lord. My soul can do some pretty fierce growling!

How about you? Does your hungry soul ever manifest physical symptoms like irritability, selfish ambitions, anger, impure thoughts, envy, resentments, and eruptions of lust?

Here's a similar analogy. Just as my mouth gets dry when I am thirsty, my spiritual mouth gets dry when I need the satisfying refreshment only God can bring.

> **After each of the following Scriptures, write the suggested symptoms of a mouth wet with God's living water.**
>
> Psalm 71:8 _____
>
> Isaiah 50:4 _____

My mouth is filled with your praise, declaring your splendor all day long (Ps. 71:8).

The Sovereign LORD has given me an instructed tongue, to know the word that sustains the weary. He wakens me morning by morning, wakens my ear to listen like one being taught (Isa. 50:4).

Our final point is very important. We can positively assume that our soul is hungry and thirsty for God if we have not partaken of any spiritual food or drink in a long while. Souls accustomed to food are more likely to have a highly developed appetite. In Psalm 63 David was accustomed to beholding the power and glory of God. He was so acquainted with God's love he considered it "better than life." Therefore, he missed God's refreshment when he didn't have it.

I think we have the same tendency. The more we've been satisfied by God's love, His Word, and His presence, the more we will yearn for it. On the other hand, we can spend so much time away from the Lord that we no longer feel hungry or thirsty. I know from personal experience that if you fail to partake of the spiritual food and drink of God for a while, you are hungry and thirsty for His satisfaction whether or not you know it!

God can satisfy your yearning soul. Satisfying your innermost places with Jesus is a benefit of the glorious covenant relationship you have with God in Christ. Open the door, Beloved! He waits to satisfy your hungry soul.

Would you end your day's assignment with a field trip? Let's call it a satisfaction field trip. Go for a walk with God. Just ask Him to fill you with a soul full of Jesus.

day four

BLESSED DISSATISFACTION

I believe God creates and activates a nagging dissatisfaction in every person for an excellent reason. According to 2 Peter 3:9, God doesn't want anyone to perish. Rather, He wants everyone to come to repentance. He gave us a will so that we could choose whether to accept His invitation, but God purposely created us with a need only He can meet.

The troubles of my heart have multiplied; free me from my anguish (Ps. 25:17).

Have you ever noticed? One of the most common human experiences is the inability to be completely satisfied. Unfortunately, salvation alone does not completely fill the need. Many come to Christ because they are seeking for something that is missing; yet after receiving His salvation, they go elsewhere for further satisfaction. Christians can be miserably dissatisfied if they accept Christ's salvation yet reject the fullness of a daily relationship that satisfies.

Do you agree or disagree with that last statement?
☐ **agree** ☐ **disagree**
Please explain your answer.

Dissatisfaction is only a terrible thing when we don't let it lead us to Christ.

Have you seen Christians who seem to have been baptized in pickle juice? We don't want to judge brothers and sisters in Christ, but do you suppose the failure to experience satisfaction in Christ might be the reason?

God offers us so much more than we usually choose to enjoy. Dissatisfaction is not a terrible thing. It's a God thing. It's only a terrible thing when we don't let it lead us to Christ. He wants us to find the only thing that will truly satiate our thirsty and hungry hearts.

To travel forward on the road to freedom, we must remove the obstacle of idolatry. We begin by recognizing the obstacle as idol worship, but we may find removing it difficult. The first two obstacles to freedom—unbelief and pride—can be removed effectively by choices we can make. We can choose to believe God, and we can choose to humble ourselves before God. I am not minimizing the difficulty, but I am suggesting the obstacles are removed by volition.

Some of the idols in our lives—things or people we have put in God's place—can take much longer to remove. Some of them have been in those places for years and only the power of God can make them budge. We must begin to remove idols by choosing to recognize their existence and admitting their inability to keep us satisfied.

The nation of Israel struggled horribly with the sin of idolatry. Isaiah recorded what he saw when he looked at Judah and Jerusalem. The passage sounds hauntingly like prosperous America. He said of the people of Israel:

> They are full of superstitions from the East;
> they practice divination like the Philistines
> and clasp hands with pagans.
> Their land is full of silver and gold;
> there is no end to their treasures.
> Their land is full of horses;
> there is no end to their chariots.
> **ISAIAH 2:6-7**

Isaiah concluded that he saw no sign of God's presence among His people. God had promised not to abandon them, and He didn't. But where sin is rampant, He is certainly capable of shrinking the presence of the Holy Spirit and leaving virtually no signs of His presence. I've experienced the withdrawing of God's obvious presence in my own life in seasons of sin.

The nation of Israel had been given everything, yet they refused to receive and be satisfied. They traded what their hearts could know for what their eyes could see. Isaiah 44:10 reminds us that a person's idols "can profit him nothing." In fact, the next verse says that idols ultimately reap shame. The chapter gives us several glimpses at the destructiveness of idols. For example, look at verse 12.

Why does the person described in Isaiah 44:12 grow faint?

People can become so engrossed in their idols that they no longer pay attention to their physical needs. Does that sound familiar?

Which of the following would be examples of neglecting physical needs because a person is seeking satisfaction from a false god?
☐ not feeding our bodies properly in an attempt to achieve a desired appearance
☐ avoiding medical care due to fear
☐ working excessive hours to achieve wealth
☐ sacrificing needed sleep to watch late-night television

Who shapes a god and casts an idol, which can profit him nothing? (Isa. 44:10).

The blacksmith takes a tool and works with it in the coals; he shapes an idol with hammers, he forges it with the might of his arm. He gets hungry and loses his strength; he drinks no water and grows faint (Isa. 44:12).

Would you agree that each of the actions above could be attempts to serve an idol rather than God? Isaiah 44:13 tells us that idols can also take the form of humans. "[The carpenter] shapes it in the form of man." We can apply this point literally. At some time each of us has exalted someone to a place where only God belongs.

Even after this catalog of idolatry, in verse 21 God promises: "'I will not forget you.'" The mercy of God is indescribable, isn't it? Even when His people turned to idols, He swept away their offenses like a cloud, their sins like the morning mist. As we face some of the idols we have worshiped in our quest for satisfaction, we need never doubt the mercy of God. He asks one thing: "return to me, for I have redeemed you" (Isa. 44:22).

Can you see the strong tie between our quest for satisfaction and the worship of idols? God created a void for Him in our lives, and it will demand attention. We desperately look for something to satisfy us and fill the empty places. Our craving to be filled is so strong that the moment something or someone seems to meet our need, we feel an overwhelming temptation to worship it.

He feeds on ashes, a deluded heart misleads him; he cannot save himself, or say, "Is not this thing in my right hand a lie?" (Isa. 44:20).

In my opinion, one of the most thought-provoking verses in Isaiah 44 is verse 20. Paraphrase the verse below.

Fresh conviction washes over me like a squall. How many times have I fed on ashes instead of feasting on the life-giving Word of God? How many times has my deluded heart misled me? How many times have I tried to save myself?

I could fall on my face this moment and praise God through all eternity for finally awakening me to say, "This thing in my right hand is a lie." I can remember one thing in particular I held onto with a virtual death grip. I also remember the harrowing moment God opened my eyes to see what a lie I had believed. I cried for days.

I originally thought this lie was a good thing. My heart, handicapped in childhood, had deluded me. Although I didn't realize it at the time, I eventually bowed down and worshiped it. My only consolation in my idolatry is that I finally allowed God to peel away my fingers. To my knowledge, I have grasped only His hand since.

Yes, I plunged to the depths to discover satisfaction. Sadly, I often learn things the hard way. I pray to settle for nothing less the rest of my days. I am very aware that Satan will constantly cast idols before me. I hope never to forget I could fall again.

Beloved, whatever we are gripping to bring us satisfaction is a lie— unless it is Christ. He is the Truth that sets us free. If you are holding anything in your craving for satisfaction right now, would you be willing to acknowledge it as a lie? Even if you feel you can't let go of it right this moment, would you lift it before Him—perhaps literally lift your fisted hand as a symbol—and confess it as an idol? God does not condemn you. He calls you. Will you open your hand to Him? He is opening His to you.

day five

CELEBRATING GOD'S "GODNESS"

Yesterday we briefly noted the difficulty of dealing with the idols in our lives. At the risk of annoying many Pharisees, I dare to suggest that you cannot simply decide to dislodge the stronghold of idolatry. Some idols have been in our lives for too long. The roots go too deep. We need a different strategy.

O Lord, you are my God;
I will exalt you and
praise your name,
for in perfect faithfulness
you have done marvelous
things, things planned
long ago (Isa. 25:1).

In the following paragraph look for reasons to take a different approach to overcoming idols.

If we confront a deeply entrenched idol directly and say, "I'm not going to do that anymore," two things happen. We develop a negative focus, and we create a satisfaction vacuum in our lives. A negative focus leads us to self-righteousness and blindness. An unmet need for satisfaction pulls us toward false solutions like iron filings to a magnet. We need to find true satisfaction to fill our unmet needs. If we try to dislodge idols in our own strength, we will become defeated and deluded. If we find satisfaction in Jesus, the idols lose their power and appeal.

Explain in your own words why we must find satisfaction in Christ to successfully overcome our idolatry.

We are practicing praying God's Word because Scripture points us to the satisfaction we can find only in God. Praying Scripture that recognizes the Godness of God is critical in the process of breaking free from strongholds. This is true for at least three reasons.

1. Virtually every stronghold involves the worship of some kind of idol. For instance, the stronghold of pride leads to the worship of self. The stronghold of addiction involves the worship of some substance or habit. Something else has become god in our lives, the object of our chief focus. We need to fill our minds with Scripture acknowledging the Godship of God as part of renewing our minds. Until we turn from our idols to God, we will never find liberty, for "where the Spirit of the Lord is, there is freedom" (2 Cor. 3:17). One missing link in almost every captive life is the spirit of God's lordship.

2. As long as our minds rehearse the strength of our stronghold more than the strength of our God, we will be impotent. As we pray the Word of God acknowledging His limitless strength and transcendent dominion, Truth will begin to eclipse the lies. We will realize that in our weakness He is strong and that as we bend the knee to His lordship, God is more than able to deliver us.

3. We may be forced to realize that our perception of God is something we have conjured up and not the one true God at all. This point may be a little hard to swallow. We may see ourselves as conventional Christians, but if we believe our God is small, that's not God at all. Truth sets us free. The truth may be that we've carved a god out of our own image, assigned him the utmost and noblest of human characteristics, unintentionally envisioning him to be more of a super human than the sovereign El Elyon—the Most High God. I am praying that we will develop a more accurate perception of God. I think sometimes God must listen to our pitifully small acclamations, expectations, and petitions in prayer and want to say, "Are you talking to Me? I'm not recognizing Myself in this conversation. Are you sure you have the right God?"

List the three reasons we need the reinforcement of praying Scripture about the Godness of God.

1. Virtually every stronghold involves ...

2. We are impotent as long as we rehearse ...

3. We need to correct our perception ...

I will never forget the story about a Sunday School teacher giving his children's class an assignment on Easter Sunday. He asked them to make an acrostic of the word *Easter*. He was stunned by one student's perception. The child had written, *Every Alternative Savior Takes Early Retirement.* What a thought-provoking statement! Hear this from a former captive: every alternative savior must take early retirement if we are ever to be free. Only one God can deliver us. The most monumental leap we take toward freedom is the leap to our knees in surrender to the lordship of Jesus Christ.

> The most monumental leap we take toward freedom is the leap to our knees in surrender to the lordship of Jesus Christ.

Please allow me the honor of leading you in a Scripture-prayer. Then choose from the suggested passages to write your own.

My Father, how I thank You that You do no wrong. You never pervert justice. Who appointed You over the earth? Who put You in charge of the whole world? If it were Your intention and You withdrew Your Spirit and breath, all humanity would perish together, and we would return to the dust (Job 34:12-15). Instead, my Lord, You have promised that Your plans for Your people are plans to prosper and not to harm, plans to give us hope and a future (Jer. 29:11).

Select one or more of the following passages and begin to build your own journal of Godness Scripture-prayers. Job 12:10; 36:26-29; Psalm 24:1; 40:5; 95:3-5; Colossians 1:15-17

_____
_____
_____
_____
_____

Week 5

experiencing
God's peace

day one

THE KEY TO PEACE

I covet for you to experience two things in this study. First, I pray for you a growing desire to live out the five benefits. So far I hope you are growing as a person whose first instinct in any situation is to believe God, a person who thinks first of His glory rather than worrying about what people think of you, and a person who finds such satisfaction in Him that false gods have as much attraction as cleaning the garbage disposal.

My second desire for you has to do with praying God's Word. Because relating to God this way has meant so much to me personally, I long for such a relationship for you. Does talking with the Father through Scripture seem less awkward for you now? I pray that you are developing through practice a prayer life you once only dreamed about.

Remember, this is a process. I have been seeking to know Christ for many years now. Don't get discouraged if things don't change overnight. I believe I can make you a promise. Stay in His Word and keep talking to Him about it. You will one day look back in amazement at the growth God has produced in your life.

Now with that pep talk behind us, let's consider *benefit 4: to experience God's peace.* I can't overemphasize the importance of peace as a real and practical benefit of our relationship with God. He does not intend for His peace to be an infrequent surprise. God wants to provide peace as the ongoing rule of our lives. The apostle Paul underscored the essential nature of peace in 2 Thessalonians 3:16.

Did you notice how crucial Paul considered peace? "At all times." "In every way." Peace can be possible in any situation, but we cannot

May the Lord of peace himself give you peace at all times and in every way. The Lord be with all of you (2 Thess. 3:16).

simply produce it on demand. In fact, we cannot produce it at all. It is a fruit of the Spirit (Gal. 5:22).

What would you call our human efforts to produce peace?
☐ stoicism   ☐ denial
☐ grin and bear it   ☐ all of these and more

To us a child is born, to us a son is given, and the government will be on his shoulders.
And he will be called Wonderful Counselor, Mighty God, Everlasting Father, Prince of Peace (Isa. 9:6).

Of the increase of his government and peace there will be no end.
He will reign on David's throne and over his kingdom,
establishing and upholding it with justice and righteousness from that time on and forever.
The zeal of the LORD Almighty will accomplish this (Isa. 9:7).

We have Christ's peace. It has already been given to us if we have received Christ. We just don't always know how to activate it. We've actually been working on this benefit from the beginning of our study as we have practiced praying God's Word. Prayer is essential to experiencing the practical reality of God's peace.

In the following paragraph look for keys to experiencing peace. Circle any key words you identify.

Isaiah uses the word *peace* 26 times. God continually promised peace when His captives wholeheartedly returned to the Lord. The familiar messianic passage Isaiah 9:6 identifies peace with Christ as "Prince of Peace." The next verse connects the Prince of Peace to His reign: "Of the increase of his government and peace there will be no end. He will reign on David's throne." Many of us have memorized the words of Isaiah 26:3.

> You will keep in perfect peace
> him whose mind is steadfast,
> because he trusts in you.
> **ISAIAH 26:3**

Isaiah 32:17 identifies yet another aspect of God's peace.

> The fruit of righteousness will be peace;
> the effect of righteousness will be
> quietness and confidence forever.
> **ISAIAH 32:17**

And who can think long about peace in the Book of Isaiah without bringing to mind the awesome prediction of Christ's suffering for us?

> He was pierced for our transgressions,
> he was crushed for our iniquities;
> the punishment that brought us peace was upon him.
> **ISAIAH 53:5**

Did you see any hints of a common denominator tying several of these Scriptures together? You could have circled words like *reign*, *government*, and *trusts*. Isaiah 9:6-7 perfectly portrays the key to peace. The key to peace is authority. When we allow the Prince of Peace to govern our lives, peace either immediately or ultimately results. Peace accompanies authority.

Have you experienced difficult times when you totally surrendered to Christ and you found that His peace transcends understanding?
□ **yes**   □ **no**
If so, what did you learn from the experience?

Peace comes in situations completely surrendered to the sovereign authority of Christ.

Can you also say, as I can, that you have had an absence of peace in much less difficult circumstances? Have you ever wondered what the difference was? I believe peace comes in situations completely surrendered to the sovereign authority of Christ. Sometimes when we finally give up trying to discover all the answers to the whys in our lives and decide to trust the sovereign God, unexpected peace washes over us like a summer rain. We sometimes lack peace in far less strenuous circumstances because we are not as desperate or likely to turn them over to God.

I finally had to turn over some of the hurts of my childhood to God's sovereign authority because I realized they would consume me like a cancer. When at last I allowed Him to govern everything about my past, not only did the Prince give me His peace, but He actually brought good from something horrible and unfair. If you have not yet bowed the knee to God's authority over areas of your past, my friend, something is holding you captive.

I hope we will be able to discover a few reasons we are so reluctant to submit to God's authority, but we must remember that bending the knee is ultimately a matter of pure obedience. You may never feel like giving your circumstance, hurt, or loss to Him; but you can choose to submit to His authority from belief and obedience rather than emotion. Obedience is always the mark of authentic surrender to God's authority.

When I finally bent the knee to the Prince of Peace over hurts in my childhood, I realized He was directing me to forgive the person who hurt me. God did not insist on my forgiving for the sake of my perpetrator but for peace in my life. Once I began to surrender to Him in this painful area, God began to give me a supernatural ability to forgive. A segment of Scripture in Isaiah beautifully reveals the relationships among obedience, authority, and peace.

This is what the LORD says—your Redeemer, the Holy One of Israel: "I am the LORD your God, who teaches you what is best for you, who directs you in the way you should go" (Isa. 48:17).

In the margin circle the titles the Lord used to refer to Himself in Isaiah 48:17.

God has a right to all authority because of who He is. Allow me to reverse the order of the titles in the verse and share my outlook on His right to complete authority. He is God, the Creator of the heavens and the earth, the supreme Author of all existence. He reigns over all and in Him all things exist. He is Lord, the Master and Owner of all living creatures. He is the Covenant Maker and Keeper. He is holy. As Lord, He will never ask anything of us that is not right, good, and open to the light. He is perfect and undefiled. Lastly, He is Redeemer, the One who bought us from sin's slave master so that we could experience abundant life. He bought us to set us free. "What, then, shall we say in response to this? If God is for us, who can be against us?" (Rom. 8:31).

Let's end our day by talking to God with His Word. Please use Matthew 5:34-35 and Luke 10:17.

_____

_____

_____

_____

_____

_____

_____   *I tell you, do not swear at*

_____   *all: either by heaven, for it*

_____   *is God's throne; or by the*

_____   *earth, for it is his footstool;*

_____   *or by Jerusalem, for it is the*

_____   *city the Great King*

_____   *(Matt. 5:34-35).*

_____

_____

_____

_____   *Lord, even the demons*

_____   *submit to us in your name*

_____   *(Luke 10:17).*

_____

_____

_____

_____

_____

_____

_____

_____

day two

WHY SO RELUCTANT?

What do you suppose would happen if we paid attention to God's commands? If we learned to live totally under God's authority? We don't have to wonder, because He told us clearly:

> "If only you had paid attention to my commands,
> your peace would have been like a river,
> your righteousness like the waves of the sea."
> **ISAIAH 48:18**

Peace I leave with you; my peace I give you. I do not give to you as the world gives. Do not let your hearts be troubled and do not be afraid (John 14:27).

Yesterday we recognized that yielding to God's authority is the key to peace. Imagine your life filled with peace like a great river.

What kinds of situations threaten your peace?

If you've ever done any boating or rafting in a river, you know what incredible power those waters contain. Many times we face situations that seem to roll over us, but we have the image reversed. God's peace is the river. The obstacles of life cannot stand against the power of God's river of peace.

I will give you three ways we can apply the image of peace like a river. In the margin beside each write how the principle could apply to your life.

1. **A river is a moving stream of water.** God's Word doesn't say peace like a pond. If we were honest, we might admit to thinking of peaceful people as boring. We may think, *I'd rather have an exciting life!* Beloved, few bodies of water are more exciting than rivers! When was the last time you saw white-water rapids? We can have active, exciting lives without suffering through a life of turmoil. To have peace like a river is to have security and tranquility while meeting

the many bumps and unexpected turns on life's journey. Peace is submission to a trustworthy Authority, not resignation from activity.

2. A river is a body of fresh water fed by springs or tributary streams. I've found that I can't retain peace in the present by relying on a relationship from the past. Peace comes from an active, ongoing, and obedient relationship with the Prince of Peace. This and other Bible studies are examples of ways God desires to feed a peaceful river in your soul.

3. A river begins and ends with a body of water. Every river has an upland source and an ultimate outlet or mouth. Rivers are fully dependent because they are always connected to other bodies of water. Likewise, peace like a river flows from a continuous connection with the upland Source, Jesus Christ, and is a timely reminder that this life will ultimately spill out into a glorious eternal life. The present life is not our destination, hallelujah! We who know Christ travel over rocks and cliffs, through narrow places and wide valleys to a heavenly destination. Until then, abiding in Christ (John 15:4, KJV) is the key to staying connected with our upland Source.

> **Which of the three images of peace seems most important to your life right now?**
> □ security in the middle of life's turmoil
> □ an active, ongoing relationship with Christ
> □ staying connected to my Source

Take pleasure in knowing that God inspired His Word with great care and immaculate precision. He chose every word purposely. When He said we could have peace like a river in Isaiah 48:18, He wasn't drawing a loose analogy. He meant it. What does it take? Attention to God's commands by obedience through the power of the Holy Spirit. Obedience to God's authority brings not only peace like a river but also righteousness like the waves of the sea. Not righteous perfection. Righteous consistency.

You see, God's way is the safe way. The right way. And the only peaceful way in a chaotic world. Beloved, I hope you've discovered that peace is not beyond your reach. It's not a goal to one day meet. You can begin a life of authentic peace today. Right now.

The path to peace is paved with knee-prints. Bend the knee to His trustworthy authority. "Let the peace of Christ rule in your hearts" (Col. 3:15).

Pray God's Word using Psalm 13:5-6; 17:6-8.

day three

OVERCOMING FEELING UNLOVED

All of us have insecurities—even the most outwardly confident people we know. Minor insecurities can be little more than occasional challenges, but when life suddenly erupts like a volcano, insecurity turns into panic. Want suddenly feels like need. A hidden pocket of unmet needs suddenly feels like a cavern. The fear or the feeling of being unloved is probably our greatest source of insecurity, whether or not we can always articulate it.

Since you are precious and honored in my sight, and because I love you, I will give men in exchange for you, and people in exchange for your life (Isa. 43:4).

God identified man's chief desire in Proverbs 19:22:

> What a man desires is unfailing love;
> better to be poor than a liar.
> **PROVERBS 19:22**

Look at the verse carefully. What in the world does being better "poor than a liar" have to do with a man's desire for unfailing love?
☐ Poor people are less truthful than rich people.
☐ Our desires make liars of us all.
☐ We lie to ourselves when we try to meet our needs with things.
☐ If we will only be faithful to God, He will provide wealth.

I believe the Holy Spirit is pinpointing the deep origin of our constant cravings to have more and more of anything. He is implying that our human tendency is to stockpile belongings or amass wealth to satisfy a cavernous need in our souls. He is also suggesting that we are lying if we say our greatest need is anything other than unfailing love. I checked the third answer.

The word *desires* in Proverbs 19:22 implies a deep craving. Each of us craves utterly unfailing love—a love that is unconditional, unwavering, radical, demonstrative, broader than the horizon, deeper than the sea. It would also be nice if that love were healthy and liberating rather than suffocating.

Our hearts are not healthy until they have been satisfied by the only completely healthy love that exists: the love of God Himself.

Interestingly, the Word of God uses the phrase "unfailing love" 32 other times, and not one of them refers to any source other than God Himself. You see, God had the transcendent advantage. Because He created us, God got to make us any way He wanted. It's not His will for anyone to perish, and because the only way to have eternal life is to receive Him, God created us with a cavernous need that we would seek to fill until we found Him.

Searching for perfect, unfailing love in anyone else is not only fruitless, but also miserably disappointing and destructive. I am convinced our hearts are not healthy until they have been satisfied by the only completely healthy love that exists: the love of God Himself. The following words by Oswald Chambers are not only written in the front of my Bible, but they are also engraved deeply in my mind: "No love of the natural heart is safe unless the human heart has been satisfied by God first."[1] We are not free to love in the true intent of the word until we have found love. In the search for unfailing love, if we unknowingly allow Satan to become our tour guide, the quest will undoubtedly lead to captivity. I know from experience.

We are not wrong to think we desperately need to be loved. We do. We are wrong to think we can make anyone love us the way we need to be loved. Our need does not constitute anyone's call but God's. Many of us have heard the devastating words "I just don't love you anymore." Others may not have heard the words, but they have felt the feeling. The fear. Throughout life we will lose to death or changing circumstances people who really loved us. As dear and as rich as their love was, it was not unfailing. It moved. It died. It changed. It left wonderful memories ... but it left a hole. Only God's love never fails. "Love never fails" refers to the *agape* love of God given to us and exercised through us (1 Cor. 13:8).

Several years ago when my heart desperately needed to be in God's ICU, He helped me picture something I believe all of us do virtually every day. We each have our unmet needs, and we carry them around all day long like an empty cup. In one way or another, we hold out that empty cup to the people in our lives and say, "Can somebody please fill this? Even a tablespoon would help!"

How do you feel about the illustration above?
☐ **Ouch! Can I ever relate!**
☐ **Not me! I don't have a cup, and I don't beg.**
☐ **Have you been reading my mail?**
☐ **I am growing less dependent on people to meet my needs.**

Whether we seek to have our cups filled through approval, affirmation, control, success, or immediate gratification, we're miserable until something is in them. I have come to dearly love and appreciate Psalm 143:8. What a heavy yoke is shattered when we awaken in the morning; bring our hearts, minds, and souls and all their "needs" to the Great Soul-ologist; offer Him our empty cups; and ask Him to fill them with Himself!

Let the morning bring me word of your unfailing love, for I have put my trust in you.
Show me the way I should go, for to you I lift up my soul (Ps. 143:8).

No one is more pleasurable to be around than a person who has had her cup filled by the Lord Jesus Christ. He is the only One who is never overwhelmed by the depth and length of our need. Imagine how different our days would be if we had our cups filled by Christ first thing in the morning. During the course of the day, anything else anyone is able to offer could just be the overflow of an already full cup. This person will never lack company or affection because she draws daily from the well of unfailing love. This blessed of all believers will know from experience what the apostle Paul meant in Colossians 2:10, "Ye are complete in Him" (KJV).

I hope you feel a need to pray God's Word right now. I think you're ready for a more thoughtful assignment. From your Bible read Proverbs 3:3-6 and talk with God about the verses. Write below any thoughts you want to retain.

_____

_____

_____

_____

_____

_____

_____

_____

_____

_____

A precious friend of mine, Danice Berger, helped me compile many of the Scriptures I rewrote into prayers in *Praying God's Word*. She was experiencing a very difficult season in which the issues of feeling unloved, insecure, and rejected were almost overwhelming. She knew the answers were right there in God's Word, but sometimes our hearts are in such pain that we resist risking exposure long enough to receive them.

Danice is a schoolteacher. She is also a serious student of God's Word. The Holy Spirit prompted me to call her and ask her to research Scripture on the topic of feeling loved and accepted by God when we are feeling unloved and rejected by others.

I have known Danice a long time, and I know she loves a good challenge; so I basically dared her to do it. She took the dare. She spent hour upon hour researching security and acceptance in the love of God. The results? Not only did she provide me with Scripture for two chapters of *Praying God's Word*, but she also received them herself. Danice did her homework ... and in the midst of it, she discovered the same unfailing love that had been there all along. This time she lifted the empty cup and let Him pour.

day four

THE OBSTACLE OF PRAYERLESSNESS

The fourth benefit of our relationship with God is to experience His peace. The key to peace is authority. Peace is the fruit of an obedient, righteous life.

You do not have, because you do not ask God. When you ask, you do not receive, because you ask with wrong motives, that you may spend what you get on your pleasures (Jas. 4:2-3).

Do you see how the benefits fit together? Which of the benefits we've studied address the issue James raised: "You ask with wrong motives, that you may spend what you get on your pleasures" (Jas. 4:3)? (Check all that apply.)
☐ **to know God and believe Him**
☐ **to glorify God**
☐ **to find satisfaction in God**
☐ **to experience His peace**

How would you explain to a new Christian how the benefits fit together to produce peace?

Did you note that benefits 2 and 3 particularly apply to the problem of asking with wrong motives? To the degree that I desire God's glory and am finding my satisfaction in Him, my motives are purified. I can ask God for great things because my desires and His are the same.

On the other hand, when we seek to glorify and satisfy ourselves, we set ourselves up for captivity. Our disobedience and rebellion against the authority of God complicate life. I can tell you from personal experience that at times of greatest captivity, I wanted more than anything to be obedient to God. I was miserable in my rebellion, and I could not understand why I kept making wrong choices. Yes, they were my choices, and I've taken full responsibility for them as my sins. However, Satan had me in such a viselike grip that I felt powerless to obey, although I wanted to desperately. Of course, I wasn't powerless; but as long as I believed the lie, I behaved accordingly.

You are probably familiar with Philippians 4:6-7: "Do not be anxious about anything, but in everything, by prayer and petition, with thanksgiving, present your requests to God. And the peace of God, which transcends all understanding, will guard your hearts and your minds in Christ Jesus."

I decided that to bring home the impact of these verses, I would have a little fun and paraphrase the passage from a negative standpoint. In other words, I turned this prescription for peace into a no-fail prescription for anxiety. My result looked like this: "Do not be calm about anything, but in everything, by dwelling on it constantly and feeling picked on by God, with thoughts like 'and this is the thanks I get,' present your aggravations to everyone you know but Him. And the acid in your stomach, which transcends all milk products, will cause you an ulcer, and the doctor bills will cause you a heart attack, and you will lose your mind."

Without a doubt, avoiding prayer is a sure prescription for anxiety, a certain way to avoid peace. To experience the kind of peace that covers all circumstances, the Bible challenges us to develop active, authentic (what I like to call "meaty") prayer lives. Prayer lives with real substance to them—original thoughts flowing from a highly individual heart, personal and intimate. Often, we do everything but pray. We tend to want something more "substantial." Even studying the Bible, going to church, talking to the pastor, or receiving counsel seems more tangible than prayer.

What victory the enemy has in winning us over to prayerlessness! He would rather we do anything than pray.

Why do you think the enemy would rather we do anything than pray?

He'd rather see us serve ourselves into the ground, because he knows we'll eventually grow resentful without prayer. He'd rather see us study the Bible into the wee hours of the morning, because he knows we'll never have deep understanding and power to live what we've learned without prayer. He knows prayerless lives are powerless lives, while prayerful lives are powerful lives!

In the following paragraph circle specific blessings that come through prayer.

In Ephesians 1 Paul prayed that his spiritual offspring would receive "the Spirit of wisdom and revelation, so that you may know him better" (v. 17). He asked God to open the eyes of their hearts so that they could "know the hope to which he has called you, the riches of his glorious inheritance in the saints, and his incomparably great power for us who believe" (vv. 18-19). The better we know God (v. 17), the more we trust Him. The more we trust Him, the more we sense His peace when the wintry winds blow against us.

Just a few days ago I again saw the best advice the world seems to have. It said, "Remember two things: (1) Don't sweat the small stuff. (2) It's all small stuff." Just once I'd like to stuff a sweaty sock into the mouth of the person who first said that, because it's not all small stuff. I have a friend whose son was paralyzed in an accident his senior year in high school. I pray almost daily for a list of people, from age 4 to 74, who are battling cancer. Two recently came off my list and into heaven. My precious friend's husband, an honest, hardworking believer with a son in college, just lost his job—again. Not long ago, three tornadoes whipped through my hometown—stealing, killing, and destroying. No, it's not all small stuff.

Worldly philosophy is forced to minimize difficulty because it has no real answers. You and I know better than the small-stuff philosophy. We face a lot of big stuff out there. Only through prayer are we washed in peace.

Only through prayer are we washed in peace.

It's time to roll away the stone of prayerlessness. It is the most prohibitive obstacle in the road to a believer's victory, no matter what our specific pursuit may be.

I believe you're ready for greater substance in your prayer life. Here is a favorite assignment of mine. Pray Psalm 86. You'll see it is custom-made for praying God's Word. Below write any insights you want to preserve from the Psalm.

_____

_____

_____

_____

_____

_____

_____

_____

_____

_____

_____

_____

_____

_____

_____

_____

_____

_____

_____

day five

ONE WAY TO PEACE

I remember a cheer popular among Christian students back in my college days. If you aren't familiar with it, you'll just have to imagine the appropriate hand gestures. It went, "One way, to peace, through the power, of the cross." The chant was trite but true. The problem is how to apply the power. Application is all about relationship, and that means prayer.

To him who is able to keep you from falling and to present you before his glorious presence without fault and with great joy (Jude 24).

Let me share with you one reason I believe prayerlessness is such an obstacle to peace. When Satan takes perfect aim at our Achilles' heel, he always picks the perfect time and wears the perfect disguise. In those times, none of the following will work effectively to keep us out of a snare:

- Discipline. Somehow, at times of great temptation and weakness, discipline can fly like a bird out the nearest window.
- Lessons from the past. Somehow we don't think that straight when we get a surprise, full-fledged attack.
- What is best for us. Our human nature is much too self-destructive to automatically choose what is best at our weakest moments.

Our strongest motivation will be the Person with whom we walk. Staying close to Him through constant communication, we receive a continual supply of strength to walk victoriously—in peace even as we walk through a war zone. Review the three elements of discipline, lessons from the past, and what's best for us. Check any of the following you have tried in a time of temptation.

☐ willpower   ☐ knowledge   ☐ enlightened self-interest

How did the solution(s) work?

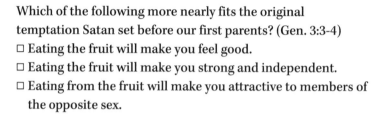

Christ came to set the
captive free. Satan comes
to make the free captive.

Beloved, let me give you another reason we need prayer as we seek to live free. Satan will try to stir up what our faithful Refiner wants to skim off. Remember, Christ came to set the captive free. Satan comes to make the free captive. Christ wants to cut some binding ropes from our lives. Satan wants to use them to tie us in knots.

> **Which of the following more nearly fits the original temptation Satan set before our first parents? (Gen. 3:3-4)**
> □ Eating the fruit will make you feel good.
> □ Eating the fruit will make you strong and independent.
> □ Eating from the fruit will make you attractive to members of the opposite sex.

Something in us makes us want to be our own boss. We don't want to need anybody. We want to be independent, but God never intended for us to be those things. He created us to be loved and to be in relationship with Him. Satan authored the "be strong" and "be independent" philosophy.

We must walk with Christ step-by-step through this journey if we are to experience His protection, power, and a resulting passion in our lives. None of these three will be realities any other way. When we get close to Christ, the enemy will be defeated. Believe it. Act on it.

Prayer matters. The Spirit of God released through our prayers and the prayers of others turns cowards into conquerors, chaos into calm, cries into comfort. The enemy knows the power of prayer. He's been watching it furiously for thousands of years. In preparation for this lesson, I searched for all the uses of the word *pray* in its various forms from Genesis to Revelation. I nearly wept as I saw hundreds of references.

> Abraham prayed. ... Isaac prayed. ... Jacob prayed. ... Moses left Pharaoh and prayed. ... So Moses prayed for the people. ... Manoah prayed to the Lord. ... Samson prayed. ... Hannah wept much and prayed. ... So David prayed. ... Elijah stepped forward and prayed. ... And

Elisha prayed, "O Lord." ... After Job had prayed for his friends. ... And Hezekiah prayed to the Lord. ... Daniel got down on his knees and prayed. ... From inside the fish Jonah prayed. ... Very early in the morning, while it was still dark, Jesus got up, left the house and went off to a solitary place, where He prayed. ... Going a little farther, He fell with His face to the ground and prayed.

If Christ sought to have the divine life strengthened in Him through solitary times of intimacy with the Father, how much more should I? I am hopeless to live the victorious life without prayer.

The Bible is a Book of prayer. And as Isaiah 56:7 reminds us, God's presence is a house of prayer. O Beloved, when our lives are over and the record of our days stands complete, may the words have been written of us, "Then he or she prayed."

Let's end this part of our study with some time praying God's Word. Record your thoughts and prayers below. Choose from the following Scriptures: Psalm 17:6-8; 25:4-7; 136; Song of Songs 2:4; Isaiah 54:10; John 15:9; 1 Corinthians 2:9. Just enjoy His presence!

_____

_____

_____

_____

_____

_____

_____

_____

_____

_____

1. Oswald Chambers, *He Shall Glorify Me* (Ft. Washington, PA: Christian Literature Crusade, 1965), 134.

Week 6

enjoying God's presence

day one

PRINTS OF HIS PRESENCE

I can hardly believe it. We've come to the final week of this Bible-study journey. I hope you have learned some things and gained some skills for living as a disciple. Much more, I hope you have come to love our magnificent God more deeply. My desire for this study has always been very practical. I've wished for you two things: 1) to burn the five benefits into your soul so deeply that ever after they will shape your motivations; 2) to develop a taste for making God's Word a vital part of your prayer life.

When you pass through the waters, I will be with you; and when you pass through the rivers, they will not sweep over you. When you walk through the fire you will not be burned; the flames will not set you ablaze. For I am the LORD, your God, the Holy One of Israel, your Savior (Isa. 43:2-3).

How have one or more of the first four benefits made changes in your life during the past few weeks?

Has learning to pray God's Word affected your experience of the benefits?
☐ yes   ☐ no
If so, describe the difference.

Benefit 5 leads us to enjoy God's presence. I doubt that any believer feels God's wonderful presence every second of every day. Sometimes we're challenged to simply believe He's with us because He promised (Heb. 13:5). That's faith.

We need to clarify what enjoying God's presence does and does not mean. Don't think because you have struggles, you are not enjoying God's presence. For example, consider that God's Word often tells us not to fear; yet not all our fears are unfounded. Think about it. Our present society poses many real threats.

> **What does the phrase "when you pass through the rivers" in Isaiah 43:2 suggest to you?**
> ☐ **God may lead me through some tough places.**
> ☐ **Walking with God will result in trouble-free living.**
> ☐ **Swimming classes start at 9:00.**

Enjoying God's presence does not mean difficult things don't happen to His children. If nothing frightening will happen to us, how can the assurance of God's constant presence quiet our fears? Psalm 139:7-12 assures us that God's presence is with us always. "Even the darkness will not be dark" to our God. Hebrews 13:5 assures us that "never will I leave you; never will I forsake you." We cannot escape God, but we do not always sense His presence.

> **From your experience with God, what are some reasons we do not always sense His presence?**

God's presence in our lives is absolutely unchanging, but the evidence of His presence varies. Sometimes God may purposely alter the evidences of His presence to bring the most benefit from our experience. We may receive the most benefit from seeing many visible prints of His invisible hands during a difficult season. Other times we may profit most from seeing fewer evidences. God does not love us less when He gives us fewer evidences. He simply desires to grow us up and teach us to walk by faith.

> **What did Jesus say to His disciples in Matthew 14:25-32?**
> ☐ **"Take courage! It is I."**
> ☐ **"Take courage! I am calming the storm."**
> ☐ **"Take courage! God is watching you."**

In the midst of a storm Jesus came walking on the water. To His terrified disciples He said: "Take courage! It is I. Don't be afraid."

But the storm continued to rage until He got into the boat. The point is not that we have nothing to fear but that His presence is the basis for our courage.

Christ does not always immediately calm the storm, but He is always willing to calm His child on the basis of His presence. "Don't worry! I know the winds are raging and the waves are high, but I am God over both. If I let them continue to swell, it's because I want you to see Me walk on the water." We'll probably never learn to enjoy our storms, but we can learn to enjoy God's presence in the storm!

In Psalm 16:11 David confidently proclaimed, "You will fill me with joy in your presence." The Hebrew word for *joy* is *simchah*, which means "glee, gladness, joy, pleasure, rejoice(ing)." We can learn to enjoy God's presence even when life is not enjoyable. I can't explain it, but I've experienced it over and over.

> We'll probably never learn to enjoy our storms, but we can learn to enjoy God's presence in the storm!

Describe a time when you have enjoyed God's presence, whether or not the circumstances were pleasant. Plan to share your example with your group.

Are you one who always needs a set of prints for reassurance? The most wonderful set of fingerprints God left with His invisible hand is probably within your reach this very moment—His Word. When it all comes down, we either choose to believe or disbelieve God. Once we choose to accept His presence as a fact, we can be free to go on to enjoyment.

Are you ready to accept His ever-abiding presence in your life as an absolute fact? Are you ready to begin enjoying God in your life more than ever? If so, take time to pray, asking Him to strengthen your faith and teach you how to enjoy Him to the fullest.

Personalize Psalm 125:1-2 into a prayer expressing your trust in God's presence.

day two

THE JOY OF RELATIONSHIP

As the deer pants for streams of water, so my soul pants for you, O God. My soul thirsts for God for the living God When can I go and meet with God? (Ps. 42:1-2).

You know I feel a closeness and affection for you that I cannot describe—even with all my adjectives! So I am going to be bold and ask you a very personal question. The honest answer to this question shapes the quality of your life more than anything I know. Do you enjoy God?

I'm not asking if you believe God (benefit 1) or if you seek to glorify Him (benefit 2). Probably, finding satisfaction in Him (benefit 3) will lead you to enjoy His presence, and certainly experiencing God's peace (benefit 4) will incline you toward Him. Ultimately, however, life comes down to whether you enjoy God.

What characteristics of God do you find enjoyable?

I love to be around people who are knowledgeable and interesting. I like people who are at least somewhat demonstrative and who care about others. I want to be around people who have something to say and who are willing to listen. I do hope you have found God to be all those things in your life.

You automatically know that I believe God is worth glorifying. One reason I believe so is because nobody satisfies the way He does. Only in His presence can you find peace in the midst of the greatest challenges imaginable.

I hope you see all that we've been doing coming together here. If you are enjoying God's presence, I want you to enjoy Him more and more. If you aren't, I see two possible causes.

You might still not believe He satisfies (benefits 1 and 3). If that's where you are, don't beat yourself up over it. Continue to get to know Him through His Word. I promise the more you know Him, the more you will believe He can meet your need.

On the other hand, you may genuinely believe God and still have difficulty enjoying His presence. Could the problem possibly be the work of the accuser? That is Satan's game, you know. Revelation 12:10 identifies him as the "accuser of our brothers, who accuses them before our God day and night."

I've said many times that Satan lacks creativity. He just keeps doing the same tried-and-false things. He wants to keep you out of God's presence, so he accuses you. He can't keep you out of heaven, but as long as Satan can keep you feeling too guilty to be in the presence of God, he wins a small victory.

On the scale below, place an X to indicate how you feel in God's presence.

●————————————————————————————————●

so ashamed I have to hide   **filled with joy**

If you have confessed and repented of known sin and still feel ashamed in the presence of the Father, something is wrong. Never in all of Scripture did Christ resist the repentant sinner. He resisted the proud and the self-righteously religious but never the humble and repentant. Indeed, forgiveness is why He came.

Some issues are more gray than others, but we've now arrived at a place we can see black and white: once true repentance has taken place, any accusation and guilt we continue to feel is the enemy. We need to be certain that we have experienced genuine repentance.

What does 2 Corinthians 7:10 tell us leads to repentance?
☐ spiritual warfare   ☐   open rebuke
☐ godly sorrow

Godly sorrow brings repentance that leads to salvation and leaves no regret, but worldly sorrow brings death (2 Cor. 7:10).

Genuine repentance does not mean merely regretting that we have sinned. Repentance comes from godly sorrow over our sin. Satanic accusation leads to crushing guilt.

Please trust me when I say that I know about this guilt issue. Satan has used guilt, condemnation, and accusation to nearly be the death of me at times. You see, I was a young child when I received Christ, and yet I have sinned and failed miserably in my life. I nearly have to fight not to be jealous over the testimonies of those who only knew the real pit of sin prior to their salvation and have walked faithfully since. Every horrible sin I've ever committed has been as a believer.

Oh, what grief strikes my heart again even as I share this testimony. As I grow to love Christ more, every now and then a wave of grief will come over me about my past sin, and I will cry to myself, *How could you have done such a thing to Him?* If I don't stop and pray immediately—restating Christ's love for me and my righteousness in Him—Satan will interpret my wave of sorrow as a vulnerability to accusation, and he will proceed with a hurricane of condemnation. I have had to become extremely proactive against his accusations. You must, too.

> **What Scriptures do you have ready to pray during times of such accusation? If you don't have a list of Scriptures, prepare one now. Plan to share your list with your group.**

You and I are about to cease cooperating with Satan's schemes. Amen? If we've never developed godly sorrow over a certain sin, let's ask God for godly sorrow. Then hang on, because He will be faithful to do it! If we have repented of sin and yet guilt keeps assailing us, let's start refusing to absorb the accuser's attacks anymore, fighting back with prayer and God's Word.

In the life of a believer, guilt experienced before we've repented of that specific sin is the conviction of the Holy Spirit. Guilt experienced after repentance is the condemnation of the evil one. Please hear this with your heart: If you have truly repented of sin, you are forgiven no matter how you happen to feel. Remember, Christ boldly proclaimed that He has "authority on earth to forgive sins" (see Matt. 9:6).

If we repent of sin and still let the evil one convince us to refuse forgiveness, what are we implying about Jesus?

Are we saying that we can do our part (repenting) but Christ can't do His part (forgiving)? I finally realized my unwillingness to accept Christ's complete forgiveness after my genuine repentance was an authority problem. I was in effect saying Christ couldn't do His job. I found myself having to repent for refusing to receive forgiveness!

Please end your day's study with a time of prayer. Let me suggest a prayer project. Begin to personalize the psalms by praying through them. For today pray Psalm 121.

day three

THE OBSTACLE OF LEGALISM

Yesterday we considered guilt as a hindrance to enjoying God's presence. Now let's change the focus just a bit to examine another aspect of the same problem.

Have you ever known someone who seemed to criticize everything you did?

☐ yes   ☐ no

How do you feel about spending time around such people?

☐ love it   ☐ can hardly   ☐ get me out
                              wait   of here

Just for the record, I know God does not act like the person above. He treats us with incomparable love and grace. Suppose, however, that you thought of God as constantly critical. How would you probably feel about Him?

Many situations or conditions can keep us from truly enjoying God's presence. For instance, not spending adequate time with Him will greatly affect our pure enjoyment of His presence. Having an underdeveloped prayer life will also rob our joy, as could harboring bitterness or anger at another person; but the person who studies God's Word in depth and experiences a consistent lack of enjoyment of God often suffers from a condition with an ugly name—legalism.

The term *legalism* does not appear in Scripture, but perfect illustrations of it are scattered throughout the Word. Numerous Scriptures teach us about legalism.

How did the Pharisees respond to Jesus healing the man with a withered hand on the Sabbath (Matt. 12:9-14)?

Why do you suppose they were so angry?

Legalists make love conditional. They have a list of requirements that must be met before God can approve of and love people. If you don't live up to the rules, you deserve to be punished, not loved. Acts 15 tells of a crucial decision in the early church, a decision that vitally affects you and me. The church was growing, and Gentiles were coming to know Christ.

What did the Pharisees say about the Gentile Christians? (Acts 15:5)
- ☐ God loves you, and we love you.
- ☐ You must be circumcised and required to obey the law of Moses.
- ☐ As you walk with Christ, the Holy Spirit will make changes in your life.

Then some of the believers who belonged to the party of the Pharisees stood up and said, "The Gentiles must be circumcised and required to obey the law of Moses" (Acts 15:5).

The leaders had to determine whether we become Christians by faith in Christ alone or by keeping the law. In the discussion that followed, Peter delivered the ultimate verdict. He said, why should we "put on the necks of the disciples a yoke that neither we nor our fathers have been able to bear? No! We believe it is through the grace of our Lord Jesus that we are saved, just as they are" (vv. 10-11).

Legalism appeared again in the Galatian churches. Teachers came telling the new Christians they must keep the Jewish law to be saved. Paul "laid down the law" on the issue.

> We who are Jews by birth and not "Gentile sinners"
> know that a man is not justified by observing the
> law, but by faith in Jesus Christ. So we, too, have put
> our faith in Christ Jesus that we may be justified by
> faith in Christ and not by observing the law, because
> by observing the law no one will be justified.
> **GALATIANS 2:15-16**

In the passages above and many others, we get a clear picture of legalism. Ecclesiastes 7:20 clearly sounds the futility of legalism.

> There is not a righteous man on earth
> who does what is right and never sins.
> **ECCLESIASTES 7:20**

Sadly, legalism didn't die with the Pharisees. Oh, that it had. I find it in others, and I find it in me. I suspect if you are honest you find it in yourself, too.

I asked earlier what would happen if someone thought God was hypercritical. We know the answer. Who wants to spend time with someone who will only pick us apart? Someone once said nagging criticism is like being nibbled to death by a duck.

Close your study today with a time of prayer. Personalize Psalm 136. First read it aloud to the Father. Then add your own verses.

day four

FAITH WORKS!

We cannot please God or find freedom in rule keeping. Never have. Never will. Tragically, self-generated righteousness will always appeal to the human heart. Yesterday we considered the potential legalist hiding in every one of us. How do we avoid the trap? In my opinion, legalism results when three conditions occur.

1. Regulations replace relationship. The Pharisees had a superficial understanding of God and no enjoyment of His presence. They threw a fit because Jesus healed on the Sabbath. The Sabbath belonged entirely to God. He established it for our benefit, not to imprison us. The greatest benefit Christ could bring to those He healed on the Sabbath was a relationship with the Savior. He initiated that relationship through healing.

> **Name some regulations your inner legalist wants to demand of others or yourself.**

I have to be careful here. I'm not advocating any form of lax discipleship. What I am saying is that rule keeping won't work. *Disciple* means *follower*. We need to become radical followers pursuing God with everything that's in us, but we must beware. A student of God's Word can squeeze the enjoyment out of his or her Christian walk by replacing relationship with regulations. Legalism also occurs when:

2. Microscopes replace mirrors. Note the words from Matthew 12:10: the Pharisees were "looking for a reason to accuse." Modern-day pharisees sometimes practice religious voyeurism, looking for a reason to accuse others. They tend to love a church "soap opera" because their own relationship with God is so unexciting. They look to the faults of others to keep things interesting.

The testing of your faith develops perseverance. Perseverance must finish its work so that you may be mature and complete, not lacking anything (Jas. 1:3-4).

Looking for a reason to accuse Jesus, they asked him, "Is it lawful to heal on the Sabbath?" (Matt. 12:10).

When we adopt the first tenet of legalism, that we can become righteous through regulations, the second follows. We start to compare our walk with others. Then we either condemn others to make ourselves appear better, or we condemn ourselves.

> **Which direction have you discovered your tendencies run apart from the work of the Spirit?**
> □ I tend to think of myself more highly than I ought (see Rom. 12:3) and therefore condemn others.
> □ I tend to get down on myself and think others are better than I am.
> □ I am ambi-guilt-strous. I can do both.

We are wise to know our own tendencies. Some of us need to be more merciful to others. Others of us need to learn to accept mercy for ourselves. Either way, the legalist prescription of rule-based righteousness will not work.

I am so thankful to testify that I have seen far more genuine examples of true Christianity in the church than unfeeling legalists. Unfortunately, I have also seen many caring Christians intimidated by the occasional full-blown legalist. Concentrating on sin can cheat a Christian of truly enjoying the presence of God. Legalism also results from a third cause.

3. Performance replaces passion. If our motivation for obedience is anything other than love and devotion for God, we're probably up to our eyeballs in legalism and in for disaster. Obedience without love is nothing but law.

> **How much do you struggle with concentrating on your performance instead of God's person?**

I've observed what I think is an amazing fact about legalism. In fact, I used that fact as the title for this next-to-last day of our study. Concentrating on our performance, striving to be good enough, perfectionism—none of these yield the desired results, but faith works! Making lists of rules to obey cannot change a human heart, but a passionate love relationship with God can transform any life. That's why I've come to believe so strongly in praying God's Word.

When you pray God's Word you build communication with the Father. You learn to think His thoughts even as you pour out your heart to Him.

I hope you have grown in knowledge through these weeks, but that was never my purpose. This Bible study is for the heart—to loosen any chains withholding the heart from enjoying the abundant liberty available in Christ's salvation. I plead with you to withhold nothing from God as you journey toward freedom in Christ.

Personalize Psalm 123 to conclude today's study, and I'll see you back tomorrow for our final stop on this journey.

_____

_____

_____

_____

_____

_____

_____

_____

_____

_____

_____

_____

_____

day five

A RADICAL WALK WITH GOD

And anyone who does not carry his cross and follow me cannot be my disciple (Luke 14:27).

I know a little of what the apostle Paul meant when he said, "I am jealous for you with a godly jealousy" (2 Cor. 11:2). My friend, I am "jealous" for you to enjoy God. I want God to be the greatest reality in your life. I want you to be more assured of His presence than any other you can see or touch. This can be your reality. This is your right as a child of God. We were destined for this kind of relationship with God, but the enemy tries to convince us that the Christian life is sacrificial at best and artificial at worst.

I tell you real freedom can be yours because I'm presently living in victory over many strongholds Satan once raised in my life. I have been for a matter of years; however, now it's up to no one else but me what my testimony will be. God has graciously allowed me a number of do-overs: hard tests I passed the second time around. I have no doubt more tests will come, but how I pray to pass them! How I pray that though I will undoubtedly stumble, I will not fall.

If we're not careful, we can respond to a season of heated warfare with legalism and religious bondage. Beware of trading one area of bondage for another!

The Book of James speaks of radical obedience. Paraphrase the following verses into prayers.

James 1:12

_____

_____

_____

James 1:21

_____

_____

_____

What does James 1:25 say the perfect law does?

A genuine walk in truth is a walk of glorious liberty! I testify with James that a radical walk with Jesus results in the greatest freedom available on the planet.

Yes, I have surrendered my life to a very radical walk with God, but I'm not miserable, nor do I fight the feeling that *this is what I get for being defeated by the devil.* I have come to a place where most often I delight to do God's will, and I see His precepts for me as green lights for victory, peace, joy, fullness, and passion. I was forced to make some radical decisions, but I wouldn't trade the relationship with Jesus Christ I discovered in my desperation for all the spotless track records in the world.

Let me be clear: I never want to go back to that kind of defeat, and I live in alertness daily. The pain was tremendous, and the cost was enormous! However, God used my defeat to bring me to a place of ministry and authenticity I would never have known.

I nearly quit ministry over the pain of past failures, which I realize in retrospect was Satan's plan. It was not until I was broken that God was released to create in me a new, healthy heart and to teach me the humility and compassion of a true servant.

I have a long way to go, but I have put the devil on alert: he may make my life very difficult, but he cannot make me quit. For I, like you, am one of God's dear children, and I have overcome the spirits of darkness because the One who is in me is greater than the one who is in the world (1 John 4:4).

I intend to continue to love God passionately and to live in the benefits of the lifestyle He gives by grace. I long to know and believe Him more every day. I want to glorify Him by all I do and say. I desire to find my satisfaction in Him, for only there will I find the longing of my soul met. As I walk with Him, I experience peace, and the crowning gift is to enjoy His presence.

In Scripture earthly marriage comes closest to picturing the reality of such a relationship. My husband, Keith, and I have been married for more than 30 years. I know my husband very well, and I believe him when he tells me something (benefit 1). In an earthly sense, I glorify him because I've lived with him so long that some of his traits now show up in me (benefit 2). He satisfies virtually every need a husband should (benefit 3). I often get to experience peace while he assumes the responsibility in matters of finances and future security (benefit 4). I could not experience the last primary benefit of our marriage without the other four, yet it is completely distinctive: I purely enjoy my husband's presence (benefit 5).

Consider your spiritual biography. Using the example of Keith and I above, describe how each benefit has played out in your relationship to God. (If you can't think of a past example, write a goal instead.)

Benefit 1: _____
_____
_____

Benefit 2: _____
_____
_____

Benefit 3: _____
_____
_____

Benefit 4: _____
_____
_____

Benefit 5: _____
_____
_____

As much as I enjoy my husband, daughters, family, and friends, no relationship in my life brings me more pure joy than my relationship with God. I certainly haven't arrived in some mystical place, nor have I made even these few steps quickly or casually. I've grown to enjoy God with time. Not every minute I spend with God is gleeful or great fun. Intimacy with the Creator grows through sharing every realm of experience. I've wept bitterly with Him. I've screamed in frustration. Sometimes I thought He was going to break my heart in two. But I've also laughed out loud with Him. Wept with unspeakable joy. Left the chair and gone to my knees in awe. Squealed with excitement. I have been to every extremity and back with God. But I would tell you that He is the absolute joy of my life. I don't just love Him. I love loving Him. Surrendering my heart to Him has not been a sacrifice.

As we end this time together, I commission you to continue your journey with Him. Pray His Word. Weep with Him and laugh with Him. Walk with Him the path of freedom.

Listen closely. The liberty bell's ringing.

HOW TO BECOME A CHRISTIAN

We are created as emotional beings capable of giving and receiving love. One of the greatest feelings we have on this earth is loving and being loved by someone else. God wants us to love Him above anyone or anything else because loving Him puts everything else in life in perspective. In Him we find the hope, peace, and joy that are possible only through a personal relationship with God. Through His presence in our lives, we can truly love others, because God is love. Love comes from God (1 John 4:7-8).

John 3:16 says, "God so loved the world that he gave his one and only Son, that whoever believes in him shall not perish but have eternal life." In order to live our earthly lives "to the full" (see John 10:10), we must accept God's gift of love.

A relationship with God begins by admitting that we are not perfect and continue to fall short of God's standards. Romans 3:23 says, "All have sinned and fall short of the glory of God." The price for these wrongdoings is separation from God. We deserve to pay the price for our sin. "The wages [or price] of sin is death, but the gift of God is eternal life in Christ Jesus our Lord" (Rom. 6:23).

God's love comes to us right in the middle of our sin. "God demonstrates his own love for us in this: While we were still sinners, Christ died for us" (Rom. 5:8). He doesn't ask us to clean up our lives first—in fact, without His help, we are incapable of living by His standards. He wants us to come to Him as we are receiving Him as Savior and Lord.

Forgiveness begins when we admit our sin to God. When we do, He is faithful to forgive and restore our relationship with Him. "If we confess our sins, he is faithful and just and will forgive us our sins and purify us from all unrighteousness" (1 John 1:9).

Scripture confirms that this love gift and relationship with God is not just for a special few but for everyone. "Everyone who calls on the name of the Lord will be saved" (Rom. 10:13).

If you would like to receive God's gift of salvation, pray this prayer:

Dear God, I know that I am imperfect and separated from You.
Please forgive me of my sin and adopt me as Your child.
Thank You for this gift of life through the sacrifice of Your Son.
I will live my life for You. Amen.

If you prayed this prayer for the first time, you are now a child of God. In your Bible read 1 John 5:11-12. These verses assure you that if you accept God's Son, Jesus Christ, as your Savior and Lord, you have this eternal life.

Share your experience with your small-group facilitator, someone in your group, your pastor, or a trusted Christian friend. Welcome to God's family!

Leader Guide

INTRODUCTORY SESSION (OPTIONAL)

Before the Session

1. Provide markers and materials for making name tags for all persons attending.

2. Plan to have workbooks available for distribution or purchase. Some churches choose to furnish books for group members at no charge. Other churches choose to allow members to pay some or all of the cost of materials. Consider the possibility that members may take the study more seriously if they share in the cost. Try to provide scholarships for anyone who is unable to purchase the book.

3. Play praise music while group members are arriving. This can also be useful to lead in worship if no one in the group is capable of directing the singing.

4. Prepare a *Getting to Know You* sheet that each participant will fill out. This sheet will provide you with information about them. It can be as simple as name, address, phone number, email, or you can make it as elaborate as you desire. The more you know, the better equipped you will be to minister to needs of group members.

5. Provide small slips of paper for participants to write out prayer requests.

6. Write the five benefits discussed in the study on poster board and hang them on the wall for the duration of the study.

Benefit 1: Know God and believe Him (Isa. 43:10)

Benefit 2: Glorify God (Isa. 43:7)

Benefit 3: Find satisfaction in God (Isa. 55:2)

Benefit 4: Experience God's peace (Isa. 48:18)

Benefit 5: Enjoy God's presence (Isa. 43:2-3)

During the Session

1. Play praise music while participants arrive. As persons arrive, introduce yourself and direct them to the nametags. Ask them to fill out the *Getting to Know You* sheet while waiting for everyone to arrive.

2. Welcome participants and tell them that you have already been praying for them and are excited they are there. This introductory session is a great time to lay a foundation for people to share with one another, to get comfortable with each other, and to establish a common goal and purpose. One way to establish a common goal or purpose

is by asking each participant what they hope to get out of this study. Always remember that there will be those in the group who are fearful of sharing openly in front of a group. Express sensitivity to that and alleviate fear by expressing that everyone is encouraged to share, but no one will ever be forced to share. Even the shy person can be brought into the discussion by asking general, nonthreatening questions.

3. Encourage participants to complete their homework in order to receive the most benefit.

4. Pass out strips of paper to each person. Ask group members to write down a prayer request for themselves, something they hope to receive from participating in this study. Fold them and pass them to the leader without names on them. The leader will read the request and pray for that individual without mentioning names.

5. Ask a volunteer to read the introduction. Ask them to underline or highlight any statements in the story that remind them of their own experience. Give them an example from the first paragraph by asking: Have you ever felt that you were failing in your attempts to please God? If so, mark that statement.

SESSION 1

Before the Session

1. Plan to provide nametags as long as everyone is still becoming acquainted. As the leader, try to have everyone's name memorized by now. Knowing their names says, "I care."

2. Provide chart paper, markers, and tape, for group presentations.

3. Write on poster board and hang on the wall the statement, *Nothing is bigger or more powerful than God! Absolutely nothing!*

During the Session

1. Have praise music playing as group members arrive. People will often come to the sessions with their minds going in many different directions. Singing or meditating on the words to a song and prayer can help refocus our attention to God and to His Word.

2. After a few moments of refocusing attention, pray for the session together. Pray specifically that members will be willing to listen as the Lord speaks to them individually.

3. Ask: What is a stronghold? Allow group members to respond. What does it mean to you to be able to exclaim, as David did, "the LORD is the stronghold of my life"? (Ps. 27:1). In response to the activity on page 8, ask members to describe a time when God kept them safe.

4. Arrange members into two groups and give each group a marker and sheet of chart paper. The group assignment is to define false strongholds and list as many as they can in five minutes.

5. Reassemble as a large group and allow each group to share their definitions and strongholds. Mount the two sheets of paper on the wall.

6. Discuss the question on page 12. Why do you think the battlefield is the mind rather than actions? Guide them to the realization that "we act out what we believe, not what we know."

7. Call attention to the poster on the wall: Nothing is bigger or more powerful than God! Absolutely no thing! Ask: Do you believe that? Why or why not.

8. Have a volunteer read 2 Corinthians 10:3-5. If different translations are available, read from them. How do we destroy arguments and pretensions? We choose truth! (p. 14)

9. Divide members into three groups. Assign each group a weapon of the world (i.e., human effort, willpower, or flesh). Ask each group to create a role play from a real-life situation where that particular weapon would be used. Be creative! After adequate time has been given, have each group present their plays.

10. Ask a volunteer to read Ephesians 6:13-18. What are the two weapons Paul lists for those in Christ? What do these two weapons do to strongholds?

11. Discuss the question on page 23, *How is intimacy with God different than the goal of being good enough to be acceptable to God?*

12. Ask a volunteer to read Romans 12:2, and ask: How are we transformed?

13. As a group, make a list of specific things you can do to "fix your eyes on Jesus, the author and finisher of your faith" (Heb. 12:2) and to "sanctify (set apart as holy) the Lord God" (1 Pet. 3:15) in your life.

14. Ask someone to read the story on page 28. How did God show His supremacy and His sufficiency?

Invite members to review the verses used in the lessons this week. Ask them to find one that is particularly meaningful to them and have each person read their verse in closing.

SESSION 2

Before the Session

Obtain small sheets of paper for group members to write Scripture prayer.

During the Session

1. Begin the session by singing praise choruses. Read aloud Psalm 34: 1-3. Ask group members to offer up words of praise, acknowledging God for who He is rather than thanking Him for what He does. Call attention to the five benefits listed on the posters located around the room. Ask members to take their Bibles and to go and stand in front of the benefit that means the most to them or the benefit they need the most right now. Look up the Scripture that applies to that particular benefit, and write your own personal prayer using that verse.

2. Allow members to pray using their own Scriptures prayers.

3. Discuss the question at the bottom of page 37, *How would you describe to a new believer the difference in believing in God and believing God?* Why is believing God such a difficult thing for believers to grasp? Ask if anyone has ever had an issue in her life that challenged her belief in God's ability or desire to help her. Would anyone be willing to share? Read together the statement on page 39, *Remember, God always wills for you to be free from strongholds.*

4. Discuss the activities on the bottom of page 40. Ask members to describe people they know who give evidence that they really know God. What makes them different from other people?

5. Ask group members to get in pairs. Have each member share briefly with her partner one life experience that has helped her learn to trust. Then, ask them to share one experience that has hindered their ability to trust. Ask members of each group to pray for one another that they will be able to grow in their ability to trust.

6. Turn to the story of Karen on page 42. Ask members what they would say to Karen.

7. Discuss the three conditions that can lead to believing God is unfaithful (p. 43).

8. Present a mini lecture on the Bible and faith. Using Hebrews 11, discuss what verses 1 and 6 have to say about faith. Take some examples of people from the Hall of Faith in that chapter and point out the consistency of God's activities in the lives of these men and women.

9. Ask for testimonies about God's faithfulness in the lives of group members. Has anyone had an experience this week that encouraged her to believe God?

10. On the back of the sheet they used earlier, ask them to paraphrase Lamentations 3:22-23.

11. Close by praying Hebrews 11:6 together. Ask God to increase your faith.

notes

SESSION 3

Before the Session

1. Pray for group members. Call or write anyone who has been absent or that God specifically lays on your heart. This will be a challenging session. Bathe it in prayer.

2. Obtain tear sheets for the planned activity.

3. Have praise music playing as members arrive.

4. Display the following statement on a marker board or poster board so that attention can be given to it the entire session. *Pride is self-absorption whether we're absorbed with how miserable we are or how wonderful we are.*

During the Session

1. As a group, read Psalm 136 as a responsive reading from NIV. Leader reads the first part of the verse, members respond, "His love endures forever."

2. After the reading, allow group members to share things that God has accomplished in their lives this past week that brings glory to Him.

3. Sing or play a praise chorus that glorifies the Lord.

4. Discuss the three possible directions our thoughts can go in the morning listed on page 51. Thinking on the cares of this world, the deceitfulness of riches, lusts of other things; pleasing God; or thinking about God's glory rather than my public image. Ask: Where do your thoughts normally go in the morning?

Possible answers, "I don't want to get up!" "What's for breakfast?" "What am I going to wear?" How can we change our thought direction?

5. On page 52, discuss the difference between humility and low self esteem. What did Isaiah say when he saw God? (Isa. 6:5)

6. Ask for responses to the statement on the board, *Pride is self absorption whether we're absorbed with how miserable we are or how wonderful we are.* Say: Most of us never associate pride with low self-esteem. What are some ways to demolish the stronghold of pride? Answers that should be included are to recognize it and pray Scripture about it daily.

7. Divide into small groups and give each group a tear sheet. List ways pride is a cheater based on Beth's ideas on page 53 and other ideas that the group may add. Assign each group one of the following Scriptures and have them write a Scripture prayer to combat pride. Deuteronomy 8:16, Proverbs 16:18, Proverbs 8:13, Proverbs 11:2, Philippians 2:3-5, 1 Peter 5:5.

8. Discuss the learning activity on page 54. What are the three key facts of God's glory? Still in small groups, have each group develop a composite definition of God's glory. Share with the entire group.

9. Ask a volunteer to read Isaiah 6:1-8. Discuss the three questions on page 55.

10. On page 57, ask group members to respond to Paul's statement in Romans 7:18, "I know that nothing good lives in me, that is, in my sinful nature." Do you agree? Disagree? Consider it a put down?

11. Discuss the learning activity on page 58. Ask: How great a part does pride play in conflict situations? Would anyone be willing to share with the group how much difficulty your pride has caused in your life? Affirm those who share. Admitting our pride is the first step to pushing that boulder out of the way.

12. As a group, respond to the activity on page 59. Describe what your life might be like if you never had to struggle with pride.

13. On page 61, discuss the question, *Why do you think God hates pride?* Ask: How do people generally view humility? As a weakness or strength?

14. Invite members to share their responses to the question or page 65. *Think back to the first person who revealed God to you. What about them made God recognizable?*

15. Conclude by affirming members for their willingness to share during this session. Share a testimony of your own experience with praying God's Word. Ask members to share experiences or insights from praying God's Word.

SESSION 4

Before the Session

1. Pray for group members. Call or write anyone who has been absent or that God specifically lays on your heart.

2. Provide tear sheets and markers for group activity.

3. Provide paper for individual activity.

4. Have music playing as members arrive.

During the Session

1. Open by asking group members to call out names of Jesus, the one who satisfies our souls. Following this time of focus, ask the group to pray the prayer on pages 73-74 together.

2. Define satisfaction. Do you agree or disagree with the statement on page 71? *Many Christians are not satisfied with Jesus.* Divide into triads. Ask each triad to make a list of evidences that someone might display who is dissatisfied with Jesus. Share lists with the large group.

3. Ask a volunteer to read Isaiah 55:1. What does God freely offer His people? Write the following statement on the board. *Christians can be miserably dissatisfied if they accept Christ's salvation yet reject the fullness of a daily relationship that satisfies.* Why is that true? Discuss what the difference is between salvation from sin and satisfaction of the soul.

4. Using the activities on pages 72-73, divide into groups of four and come up with a top 10 list of why you "can't get

no satisfaction" from these things (i.e., Manicures and pedicures only last so long!) Give five minutes and come back to the large group to share. Make this a fun activity!

5. Discuss the definition of *idol*. As an individual activity, have group members list any false gods or idols that they have placed in their lives. Assure them that this activity is personal and will not be shared. Remind the group of what they studied this week, that the way to remove idols is by choosing to recognize their existence and admitting their inability to keep us satisfied. Ask: What is the danger of worshiping idols? It takes our focus off of God. Pray 1 John 1:9 as a prayer and challenge group members to claim this verse for themselves. As a visual reminder that God is faithful to forgive and cleanse us, ask them to tear their lists to shreds and throw them away.

6. Discuss as a group why we must find satisfaction in Christ to successfully overcome our idolatry. (pages 76-77)

7. On page 86, discuss the three reasons we need the reinforcement of praying Scripture about the Godness of God.

8. Conclude by asking group members to choose one of the Scriptures on the bottom of page 87 and read as closing prayers.

notes

SESSION 5

Before the Session

1. Pray for group members. Call or write those who have been absent.

2. Enlist a group member to share a testimony about experiencing peace in the midst of a storm.

3. Discuss plans for a time of celebration next week as the study ends. Suggestion a time of fellowship with snacks or a meal together. This will be a time to celebrate what God has done in the lives of group members during the study.

During the Session

1. Have music playing as group members arrive.

2. Begin by reading Isaiah 26:3. Discuss what it means to have a steadfast mind. Play music for a time of quiet meditation asking members to keep their minds steadfast on Him.

3. As a group, share answers to the question on page 91: *Have you experienced difficult times when you totally surrendered to Christ and you found His peace transcends understanding? What did you learn from the experience?* Ask, Have you experienced absence of peace at times? Compare the two situations. What did you do differently?

4. Divide into two groups. Have group 1 discuss and list ways God's authority affects peace in our lives. Have group 2 discuss and list ways obedience to God affects peace in our lives. Share the lists in large group.

5. Ask a volunteer to read Isaiah 48:18. Discuss the question on page 94: *What kinds of situations threaten your peace?* Discuss the three ways to apply the image of peace like a river. How do these apply to our lives?

6. Make two separate lists on the board. List 1 for insecurities people can possess. List 2 for ways to overcome insecurities.

7. Based on Proverbs 19:22, what is man's chief desire? Discuss why no human being can fill the need we all have to be loved. Many times we "look for love in all the wrong places." What are some of those places? What did Paul mean in Colossians 2:10 when he said, "and in Him you have been made complete?" (NASB)

8. Ask members to pair up with another person. One person plays the role of a new Christian. The other person explains how the four benefits we have studied fit together to provide peace. Then change roles.

9. Ask a volunteer to read Ephesians 1:17-21. List on the board or a tear sheet the specific blessings that can come through prayer.

10. In week one, Beth made the statement, "Prayerless lives are powerless lives and prayerful lives are powerful lives." Do you agree or disagree? Why or why not? Ask members to share examples of times they have used willpower, knowledge, or enlightened self-interest

in times of temptation (p. 105). How did the solution work?

11. Conclude by singing the words to the first verse of the hymn, "What a Friend We Have in Jesus."

> *What a friend we have in Jesus,*
> *All our sins and griefs to bear!*
> *What a privilege to carry*
> *Ev'rything to God in prayer!*
> *Oh, what peace we often forfeit,*
> *Oh, what needless pain we bear,*
> *All because we do not carry*
> *Ev'rything to God in prayer.*
> **Joseph Scriven**

12. As members leave, ask them to write Scripture prayers from verses that have been meaningful during the study and bring them next week.

SESSION 6

Before This Session

1. Prepare in advance for a time of celebration. Pray that God would seal this study with His blessings.

2. Secure tear sheets for group assignments, index cards and stationery with envelopes for individual assignments, and a candle.

During the Session

1. Have music playing as the group enters.

2. Sing a hymn or worship song to open the session. Spend time in prayer thanking God for what He has accomplished in the lives of the group members during this six-week study.

3. Share testimonies from the questions on page 109, *How have one or more of the first four benefits made changes in your life during the last few weeks? Has learning to pray God's Word affected your experience of the benefits? If so, what difference has it made?*

4. Divide into groups of 3 or 4 and list some reasons, based on your experience, why we do not always sense His presence. Share these lists with the entire group.

5. Ask a volunteer to read Matthew 14:25-32. Challenge the group to meditate on His presence as you play a worship song or instrumental music.

6. Look on page 111 and have group members describe times when they have enjoyed God's presence, whether the circumstances were pleasant or not.

7. Discuss the question on page 112, *What characteristics of God do you find enjoyable?*

8. Give each member an index card. Using the learning activity on page 114, compile a list of Scriptures to pray when the "accuser of the brethren" accuses you. Write down the verse on the card. Suggest that they carry these verses in their purses or pockets so that they are available at all times; and when the enemy attacks, they will be ready to fight using TRUTH.

9. Discuss the affect legalism has on our enjoying God's presence. On pages 119-120 discuss the conditions that characterize a legalist. Give examples of each.

10. Ask members to share examples of how they have experienced the five benefits played out in their relationship to God.

11. Conclude in a time of worship. Place the candle in the center of the room. Give each member a piece of stationary and an envelope. Ask them to write a letter to God expressing thanks for what He has done in their lives and also committing to pray Scripture concerning areas that still may be a stronghold. Encourage them to pray Scripture as they write the letter. Give instructions beforehand so this time can be one of uninterrupted worship. Ask members to take the letters they have written and pass

them around the group asking the other members to sign their name to each letter. When letters are returned to their owners, ask members to come forward as you, the leader, take the candle and seal the letter with wax. Suggest that they keep this letter in their Bibles as a constant reminder of the changes that have taken place in their lives and the commitments made. Choose a song of commitment to play during this worship time.

Stop by Our Online Home

We have resources to help you grow in your faith, develop as a leader, and encourage you as you go. Visit us online to find Bible studies, digital downloads, events, and more!

lifeway.com/women

LifeWay | Women